The Brown Bag

The Brown Bag

a bag full of sermons for children

by

Jerry Marshall Jordan
Illustrated by Mary Lou Anderson

The Pilgrim Press
New York/Philadelphia

The poem on page 77 is reprinted by permission of Random House, Inc. from *Dr. Seuss's ABC*, © copyright 1963, by Dr. Seuss.

"Dennis the Menace" cartoon courtesy of Hank Ketcham and © by Field Newspaper Syndicate. T.M.*.

Library of Congress Cataloging in Publication Data

Jordan, Jerry Marshall, 1937-
    The brown bag.

    (A Pilgrim book)
    1. Children's sermons.   I. Anderson, Mary Lou.
II. Title.
BV4315.J68 1977   252'.53   77-16813
ISBN 0-8298-0340-8

The Pilgrim Press, 287 Park Avenue South, New York, New York 10010

To Gayle
For Tap and Suzanne

Contents

The Brown Bag

Preface

" "I wasn't taught that in seminary, but I'll try." That's how it began for me. Two concerned mothers had requested sermons for their children and the other children in the church. However reluctant I may have been at that time, I since have become convinced that sermons especially for children should be an essential part of the church's ministry. We have too long underestimated the ability of children to grasp important concepts, provided the concepts are presented in language they can understand and at their level of experience. Furthermore, concepts acquired early in life have a durability that is both promising and frightening. We ought to do what we can to capitalize on the promise.

This collection of sermons for children was used in two churches, Columbia United Church of Christ, Columbia, Missouri and the First Congregational Church of the United Church of Christ, Colorado Springs, Colorado. The members of these two congregations have been very supportive of these efforts.

Ever since I began preaching sermons for children I have used a brown bag to carry the prop used in illustrating each sermon. Quite by accident, it has become my trademark. I am often asked when I arrive at church on Sunday morning with my bag in hand, "What do you have in your bag this morning?" My reply is always the same: "Wait and see." The advantage in using the bag is that it builds a sense of anticipation in the children, causing them to be ready listeners before I have ever said a word. Thus, the title of this book, *The Brown Bag,* seemed a natural one, especially after Gayle suggested it.

Thanks go to Joan Bentlage and Ann Smith for first suggesting that I undertake sermons for children. Also, thanks to Dr. P. Roy Brammell and Jean Peterson for suggestions on the preparation of the manuscript for publication. To Mary Lou Anderson, who shared her artistic abilities by illustrating the props I used for these sermons, and to my secretary, June Winter, who typed the manuscript with great care, my sincere thanks. But most of all, thanks to Gayle for being the right person at the right time in my life to inspire me in this great task of preaching, even to the young among us. Our two children, Tap and Suzanne, also deserve thanks for adding their lively and often important touches to these sermons for children.

No. 1

Developing

Hold it. Don't move. Smile. I want to take your picture. That's right, I want to take your picture this morning. I'm ready, are you? But where is my camera? You guessed it; it's in my brown bag.

How many of you have ever seen this kind of camera? Nice-looking, isn't it? But there is more than looks to this camera, which you will soon see. It's called an SX-70 Polaroid. I borrowed it from a friend. This is how you open it. And what's so special about this camera? Besides looking nice and taking good pictures, it also develops the pictures, which makes it different from other cameras. And how does it do it? That question is most easily answered by taking your picture right here and now.

Ready? Hold it. Don't move. Smile. . . . There we are. Wait a minute; let me take another one. . . . Now let's see what the pictures look like. You don't see anything, do you? The pictures are all grayish looking. But if we wait about a minute, we'll begin to see something showing, even if it is ever so faint. Then if we wait another couple of minutes, right before our eyes we'll see these pictures develop fully. As we watch it, it will get clearer. . .and clearer. . .and clearer. At last the pictures will be finished. It's truly marvelous!

As you watch this happening, I will have to say that I don't know how the picture develops. If we really want to know, we'll have to ask the people who make this kind of

13

camera. But it does it nevertheless, and we'll soon have these pictures fully developed to prove it.

Notice that, as we've been talking, these pictures have begun to look more like they should. In watching them develop, I'm reminded of how this is like us. You see, when the camera shutter snaps and the bulb flashes, the picture of us is taken. However, at first we don't see what has happened. But the possibility of this picture appearing is there, and given time it comes out clearly. So, as time goes by, the picture begins to appear, becoming clearer and clearer until we are shown with all our vivid colors at last in view. Now this happens as it should when the film has been properly exposed (that's when the camera shutter opens and the film sees what it is made to see). Thus it is with life.

We have been exposed to God's love. At first we don't understand what it all means. But the "image" of God is within us. Then the developing process begins. We grow up, and our lives become a clear picture. Why? Because we have been exposed to God's love, and we are developing as God wants us to. It's truly marvelous when this happens!

Now I'm going to take another picture of you. It will develop like the others did. And as you think about it, I want you to remember that this picture is like our lives, for even now we are in the process of developing into what God wants us to be like. And that should really cause us to smile.

Ready? Hold it. Don't move. Smile.

P.S. (that means one more thought): These pictures will be posted on the church bulletin board for you to look at immediately after this worship service.

Let us pray.

Dear God: May our lives become a picture which shows your love. Amen.

No. 2

A Super Sunday

A lot of people have been waiting many weeks and months for today. For them, today is special. It's a "super" Sunday.

Some of you know what I'm talking about. Certainly your parents know what this is all about. This is the big day of professional football. It's time for the Super Bowl. I'm ready. I have my football with me, or I should say, my son's football. And out of the bag it comes.

Today two teams will play the best they can, each hoping that it will be good enough to win. Not only is winning quite an honor, but the players earn a lot of money if they win—or even if they don't win. In order to be able to play in the Super Bowl, the members of these two teams had to put forth a super effort. They had to work hard in practice, listening carefully to what the coach was telling them to do. Then all season long, from mid-August to mid-December, they put into practice what they had learned. In other words, they had to play hard and get better and better in order to win their games and get a chance to play in the Super Bowl on Super Sunday.

You may not think of yourself as a football player; you may not even grow up to be a football player; you may not even like football (some of you are nodding your heads that this is true). But even so, today can be a super Sunday for all of you, and for me too. In fact, each Sunday of the year can be a super Sunday. How can we make it so? You are the team and I'll be the coach; I will tell you two ways to make each Sunday a super Sunday.

15

The first way is to work hard during the week. I want my team to work hard at being good to others every day of the week. When you help others play the game of life better, you'll find that you are winning the game of life yourself. If you want to feel super on Sunday, just try being good to others all week.

The second way to make every Sunday super is to prepare yourself for Sunday so that you can really come to worship God. I've heard people say on Sunday, "I didn't get a thing out of church this morning," which has caused me to say to myself, "Well, maybe you didn't come prepared to get anything out of church." If you will worship God as you should—and, of course, this doesn't mean you are to worship God only on Sunday—you will prepare yourselves by reading the Bible, by praying each day, and by listening for the ways God speaks to you to tell you what you should do.

So, team, there are two things to do to make every Sunday a super Sunday: give loving help to others during the week, and then prepare yourselves every day of the week to say to God, "I love you."

When you and I do this, we will be doing what God, the owner of our team, wants us to be doing, and our Sundays will really be super.

Let us pray.
Dear God: We want this and every Sunday to be super. Amen.

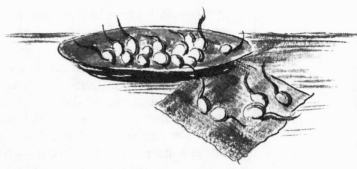

No. 3

Full of Beans

I love Chinese food. Just saying this makes my mouth water.

How many of you like Chinese food? Ah, more of you raised your hands than not, and that's good. And it's good for you too. Perhaps you've eaten it at a Chinese restaurant, or you may have eaten it at home. Some of you may have seen it prepared at home. If so, you know that many good things go into it, like many different kinds of vegetables, rice, eggs, and meat, depending of course on what kind of Chinese dish is being prepared. But there is one thing that goes into almost every Chinese dish, and this has really caught my interest. They're called bean sprouts.

We used to buy bean sprouts in the grocery store, but not anymore. Now we grow them at home. In fact, the ones we grow at home taste much better than the ones we used to buy. You're probably thinking that we grow these in our garden. Not so. Would you believe that we grow them in our kitchen? We do. We have some growing now. I've brought them along this morning in my brown bag to show you what they look like. They are in this dish with a lid, and they are covered with this wet paper towel. Here they are.

The kind of beans I'm sprouting are called mung beans. When I use the word sprouting that means they are beginning to grow. Notice how these beans are coming out of their hulls, how they are sending forth those little white roots. When those little white roots are about an inch and a half long, the bean sprouts are just right to eat.

It takes about four or five days to sprout these beans so that they are ready for eating. After we had washed the beans, we kept them in a dark, moist place. That's why they are in this dish with a lid on. They are kept moist with a wet paper towel over them. Twice a day, in the morning and in the evening, we washed them off with cool water. In the meantime, we waited for the beans to grow. And, when they are ready, we'll eat them. As you can see, these beans aren't quite ready yet—another day ought to do it. And how will we eat them? In Chinese food, of course! But, I might add, they can be eaten in other ways, like in salads, in casseroles, by themselves—and I read where one expert on bean-sprouting suggested "Sprout Ice Cream" (but surely that person was joking!).

Every time I look into this dish at these beans, a special thought comes to me, and it's not just about eating. Rather, I marvel at the wonder of it all. New life is unfolding right before my eyes. Let me quickly say that even though I added water to these beans I'm not responsible for what is happening. Sure, I'm helping it to happen. If I had kept them in the plastic bag up on the shelf away from the water, they wouldn't have grown. But even though I supplied the water, I must never forget that it's God who is causing all this to take place. That's what I think about as I watch these beans sprout.

Then I look all around me in this world at how life is happening. From grass to trees, from puppy dogs to people, the miracle of life is occurring all the time. It's truly wonderful! And God is the one who planned it this way.

In my brown bag I also have more mung beans in small plastic bags, ten beans to each bag, for you to take home and grow. Instructions on how to grow them are enclosed. Your parents can help you. As you do it, I want you to think about the miracle of life God is performing with these beans and in all of life around you, including yourself. Next week tell me how your beans grew and what your thoughts are about God as a life-giver.

Let us pray.

Dear God: Thank you for the miracle of life. Amen.

18

No. 4

Hurting Without Knowing

Several weeks ago I went to a wedding. The night before the wedding there was a rehearsal where the woman and man practiced getting married. After the rehearsal I was invited along with a lot of other people over to the home of the groom's parents. I had a wonderful time, with good food and good conversation.

During the evening I began talking with the groom's father about his hobby. Beside his house he had built a hothouse, a glass-enclosed room in which to raise plants. It was really something. He had more kinds of plants in there than I can possibly name or remember. But two of them I do remember: a banana tree and an orange tree. And what do you know, he gave me a small orange tree that had started from a seed he had planted. I felt very honored and pleased. I had never had an orange tree before. Want to see it? It's right here under my brown bag.

If you will look closely, you will see that something is wrong with this little tree. Look at the leaves; they are all curled up. Let me tell you what happened.

As I left their house, the temperature was around zero—I think it was just a little below zero. There was snow on the ground, and it was cold, cold, cold. I hurried to the car, thinking that the short way I had to go from the house to the car wouldn't hurt this little tree. But it did, and I didn't know it at the time.

The next morning the leaves looked like they do now, all curled up. I thought

19

maybe it just needed water, but watering didn't help. Then I was told by a friend that too much water would hurt it. So I let several days go by without watering it, and it didn't get better. I worried and worried about it. What could I do to make it look healthy again? Then it dawned on me what was wrong. The tips of the leaves had been frozen. No, they aren't frozen now, but they froze when I raced to the car on that cold night. Without knowing it, I hurt this little orange tree.

Sometimes, it's the same way with people. Often we hurt people without knowing it. Of course, there are other times when we do really mean to hurt someone, and that's bad. But so often we hurt others unknowingly.

Recently I had a person complain to me that I had given her the cold shoulder. That means that I was not as friendly as I should have been. Thinking back to the time I had met this person, when it was reported that I had been unfriendly, I honestly do not remember trying to be that way. I was in a big hurry then, late for a meeting. Maybe I did give her the cold shoulder. I told her I was sorry and that I didn't mean to hurt her feelings.

We should always ask ourselves what we are doing to those around us. Are we hurting them in some way like the little orange tree was hurt by the cold? An honest answer may make us more loving and careful of others. That's what Jesus would have us do. He gave us a good rule to follow: "Always treat others as you would like them to treat you." If we do this we'll all be happier because we won't be hurting one another.

I hurt this little orange tree because I wasn't quite careful enough with it, and that makes me sad. If I'm not careful, I might hurt other people without even knowing it. If we have an orange tree, or any plant worth caring for, let's take extra good care of it. When it comes to people, let's all try to treat them as we should—with loving care.

Let us pray.
Dear God: Help us to be more loving and careful of others. Amen.

No. 5

It's a Puzzle

What I want to talk about this morning is a real puzzle. No, I'm not puzzled about what I want to say. Rather, the item in my brown bag is a real puzzle, and here it is. As you can see, it's all put together. It was completed with the help of some friends. Some masking tape was put on the back to hold it together.

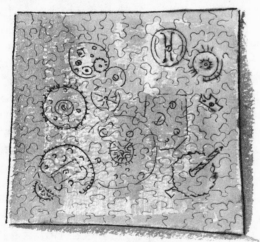

I gave this puzzle to Gayle for her birthday. Last Monday she started putting it together. Well, I just had to sit down and help find the pieces that fit. I always start with the borders; they are the easiest with those straight edges. But once we had done that (and would you believe we couldn't find three of those border pieces until more than half of the puzzle was put together?), we found out that this was the hardest puzzle we had ever done. As you can see from the picture, it's like looking inside a watch repairer's drawer, with hundreds of watch parts thrown together. Most confusing!

As we worked on it, it struck me how much life is like a jigsaw puzzle. We start life with a picture of what it should be like, a picture described by our parents, our friends, and our world. Granted, in real life we cannot see ahead of us all the details of what it will look like, but we get a fairly good idea. But then we soon realize that we have to put that life together, piece by piece. It's hard! It takes time. And there are times when we don't know if all the pieces are going to fit together. With each piece we put into place, the picture becomes a little clearer. So goes life.

When we were having the most trouble putting this puzzle together, I mentioned that we just had to get this puzzle done by today, since I wanted to show it to you. Well, after choir practice Gayle brought home four persons who had volunteered to help. With plenty of popcorn, and good music on the stereo, they helped us complete this puzzle. You know, that's the way life is. At times we need the help of others. When we need it, how great it is to be able to turn to someone and seek his or her assistance.

Have you ever finished putting a jigsaw puzzle together, only to find that the last piece was missing? That happened to us too. So we all got down on our hands and knees to look under the table and chairs. Yes, as you can see, we found it (don't ask me which piece it is). It was under my chair. Having found it, I had the privilege of putting in place the last puzzle piece. But as it is in real life, sometimes that missing piece cannot be found. What then? Then we turn to God, the maker of life's puzzle, and we ask for help in making our lives complete. And we know that God can and will help us.

All this came to mind as I puzzled this week. I ask you, isn't this the way life is?

Let us pray.
Dear God: We need your help to put it all together. Amen.

22

No. 6

AH-CHOO

Excuse me for a moment. . . .
I just had to do that. My nose just had to be blown.
Yes, I've got a cold. That's why I've brought my tissue
box in my bag. This is no put-on. I really do have a cold.

It started last Friday evening. The first sign was a
slight tickle in my throat. I was here at the church for a
wedding rehearsal. My first thought was that maybe I had
strained my voice in telling everyone where to stand and
what to do at the wedding. But that usually doesn't
happen to my throat when I'm telling people how to get
married. I speak softly to them. Really I do! Well, as the
evening went on, I knew that it must be a cold coming on.
And my second thought was right.

I spent most of yesterday—Saturday—in bed. After
breakfast I went right back to bed, and I did the same
after lunch. Why? Because I didn't feel very well. My
throat was much sorer. My head felt like a big
marshmallow. When asked how I felt, I replied with one
word, "Augh." Translated, that means "terrible." You
who have had a bad cold and all that goes with it, you
know how I felt.

As I lay in bed, I had two main thoughts. The first
was about this morning. I just had to get better! If I felt this
morning like I did yesterday, or even worse, should I try
to come to church? If I didn't come, who would take my
place—at such a late notice? I was told in no uncertain
words that if I felt this bad on Sunday or if I got a fever
(which I didn't have then), I wasn't going. Furthermore, I
was told, "The people there don't want your cold or

whatever else you have." Lying in bed, I thought about this, and I concluded that that was right.

The second thought had deeper significance, and it is what I want you to remember this morning. As I lay in bed, I didn't feel very religious. Already I've told you how I felt: "Augh." What this means is that God wasn't very much a part of my thoughts then. God didn't seem all that near to me. This low feeling didn't help. Of course, I still had the wedding to perform (which was last night), and I still had some work to do on my sermon for this morning. (When your parents hear what I have to say to them this morning, some of them may conclude that I must still be sick.) What concerned me a great deal was not just in getting the wedding taken care of (which I did in spite of my cold), but how I was to finish writing my sermon feeling like I did. But I did finish it. How?

The first thing I did was take the medicine I was supposed to take. Then I gargled a lot. When I knew I could stay in bed no longer, I got up and went to work. It wasn't easy, but it had to be done. But the main thing that helped was something I learned a long time ago. Just because I felt terrible and couldn't feel very near to God, this didn't mean that God was far away. In other words, my faith in God doesn't depend on how I feel at any particular moment or on any certain day. God is with me in spite of how I feel. This I knew without a doubt as I got up to finish my preparation for this morning.

This is something we all need to remember. God is with us always—in sickness and in health, in good times and in bad times. Yes, God is with us, regardless of how we feel. Oh, by the way, I feel better today than I did yesterday.

Let us pray.
Dear God: Thank you for being near to us in spite of how we may feel. Amen.

No. 7

I'm at Your Disposal

Here it is again—the week of love. It's time to send valentine cards. How many of you are planning to give or send valentine cards to those you especially like? I've been doing this for years and years, as far back as first grade and maybe even before that.

Sending or giving valentines is a wonderful thing. In short, it says that the person you're directing your attention to is extra special. Would you believe that I'm still sending valentine cards? I am. Yes, one is being sent to my mother, for to me she is very special. But there is another person in my life who is very, very special—my wife. I will also give her a valentine card. I give her one every year. On this February 14th I'll give it to her and it will say, "I love you."

Would you believe that she has saved many of the valentine cards I've given to her over the years? She has. In fact, I recently ran across some of them. There is one in particular that she tells me she really liked. I've brought it this morning in my brown bag. Would you like to see it?

This card is part of an inside joke. An inside joke is a joke understood by just a few people. This joke is between the two of us. I don't think she will mind if I share it with you.

We have a waste disposal unit in our kitchen and the wrong things keep trying to go down into it, mainly dishcloths. Of course, when a dishcloth goes down it gets all tangled up in the disposal, causing it not to work. Time and again, I have been called on to fix it. And so it says on this funny valentine card, "I'm at your disposal." There's a man working on the disposal with only his legs and feet sticking up. Funny, isn't it?

But what this card says that really counts is what I wrote on the inside. Now this is rather personal. I hope she won't mind if I share it with you. But let's keep it just between us, OK? It reads "Dear Gayle, I love you. . .forever. . . .Love, Jerry."

That's what God says to us too. "I love you. . .forever." And that's not just for one day out of the year, like on February 14th, Valentine's Day. God's love is for every day of the year, for every year of our lives, and even beyond our living in this world—forever.

How do we know this? Because God has sent us a personal message of love through Jesus. And it says, "I love you. . .forever." In the Bible it is said this way, "For God so loved the world that he gave. . . ." Gave what? Love through Jesus!

That is the best message we have ever received. Let's not forget it.

Let us pray.
Dear God: Thank you for your message of love through Jesus Christ. Amen.

No. 8

How Do You Measure Up?

Out of my brown bag comes a yardstick. I don't know if a yardstick does much for you, but it does a lot for me. You know what it is for, don't you? Measuring things, of course. I have seen them used in other ways,

such as for spankings. (Let me say that that use of the yardstick should be ruled out.) A yardstick has three feet to its credit—thirty-six inches. In my lifetime I would venture to say that I have literally measured miles with one.

But the one thing I remember most about a yardstick is being measured myself. There was a time when I was as tall as you. Occasionally my parents or grandparents would want to see how tall I was. So they would back me up to the wall, or to the door, and mark lightly with a pencil where the top of my head came. Then they would have me stand aside while they measured. We had a certain door on which those pencil marks stayed, and again and again they would measure how I, as well as my sister and brother, had grown over the years. Maybe that is where the question "How do you measure up?" came from.

Well, how *do* we measure up? Aside from learning how tall we are, we need to know what kind of person we are. How do we measure that? Not with a yardstick made of wood or any other material like it. Rather, we must ask the questions that measure our hearts and minds. For example:

How kind are we to others, especially when they are not very kind to us?

How patient are we when things aren't going our way?

How understanding are we when things go wrong because someone didn't know better, or maybe because they did know better but didn't want to do better?

How loving are we when love is needed to help another person whose life has grown difficult?

How reliable are we when someone is counting on us?

How good are we when no one is looking?

Yes, questions like these are a bit different from those that can be answered by a yardstick. Both are measures, but they measure different things

I hope you become as tall as you would like to become. But even more important, I hope you become big persons in *here,* in your hearts and in your thoughts. And this means that I hope you become all that God wants you to become, with love as the rule of your lives.

How do you measure up?

Let us pray.

Dear God: We want to be big persons where it counts—in our hearts and thoughts and lives. Amen.

No. 9

Feed My People

In my big brown bag, I have a little brown bag. And in this little brown bag I have something I want you to have. It's dry, hard bread. Here, try some.

How did it taste? Like dry, hard bread? Sure, that's what it is. Now you would like to have something to drink, like milk, wouldn't you? But I don't have any milk. Nor do I have anything else for you to drink or eat with this dry, hard bread. That's all you can have.

How would you feel if that were all you could have to eat today? Hungry? Then what if that were all you could expect to eat tomorrow, some more dry, hard bread? Your hunger pangs would become sharper, sharper, and sharper. If this were all you had to eat day after day, week after week, you would no doubt begin to wonder if you could continue to live. It's a simple fact of life—if you don't eat enough, you starve; and if you starve long enough, you die.

There are a lot of people in our world who have to face this fact of life every day because they don't have enough to eat. It's not something I like to think about, but it's true nevertheless. Every day this happens to people, up to five hundred million of them, more than half of them children. It's so sad. The more I read and hear about this problem, the more I'm convinced that we all need to work harder to help those who are starving in our world.

Why are there so many people who are starving? There are plenty of reasons, like bad weather keeping the necessary food from growing, or people not having enough money to buy the food they need, or the people who have food not sharing it with those needing it so badly. Of course, there are other reasons people continue to starve each day, but they all come down to one basic fact: too many people each day don't have enough food.

Some of us who see this problem and feel bad about it want to say to God, "Why have you let this happen?" God answers this question with another question directed to us who have plenty of food: "Why do you *let* it happen?" God also says, "Feed my people," ever trying to get us to understand that it is possible to grow enough food to feed everybody if we will share it as we should. God wants us who have so much to share with those who have so little.

This is where our problem begins—with people who don't understand what it means to share like this. It should make us sad and mad. Most certainly it makes God sad and mad. But I want to report to you that more and more people are becoming aware that we who have so much must join together to share our food with those who don't have enough. The more we do this, the happier they are, the happier we are, and the happier God is.

Maybe your parents already are giving to help the hungry. The church is trying to help hungry people all over the world. So is our government. You may want to talk with your parents or church school teacher about how you together can help some of those who are starving, help them have more to eat than just some dry, hard bread.

Let us pray.
Dear God: We want to help the hungry people of the world. Amen.

No. 10

Hot-cross Buns

How many of you have ever eaten hot-cross buns? I can tell by the look on some of your faces that you don't know what hot-cross buns are. Well, now is the time to learn about them.

In my children's Mother Goose book there is a rhyme about them. Maybe you've heard it before. It goes like this:

> Hot-cross buns! Hot-cross buns!
> One a penny, two a penny, hot-cross buns.
> If you have no daughters, give them to your sons.
> One a penny, two a penny, hot-cross buns.

Perhaps a good way for you to know what hot-cross buns are is to have one this morning during the fellowship time after this worship service. The Senior High Fellowship has made them and they will be sharing them with the congregation then. The senior highs decided that this was a good thing to do for the first Sunday in Lent (Lent is a forty-day period before Easter). I personally think it is a good idea, for already they have allowed me to sample what they baked. Very good!

What are hot-cross buns! I've brought one in my bag. Here it is. It's a sweet bun with a white cross made of icing on it.

Who thought of making the buns this way? Well, it didn't begin with our senior highs. It's been done for thousands of years.

For example, the early Greeks and Romans, even before Christianity came into being, ate bread marked with a cross, with the cross representing the four quarters of the moon. The people of early England, people called the Saxons, ate crossed bread in honor of their goddess of light. More recently the Mexicans had a similar custom. There are many more examples of people putting crosses on their bread, with as many reasons for doing it as there are examples.

The church did it too, but for another reason. The cross here stands for the cross on which Jesus died. It reminded them of Jesus' willingness to die to tell people about God. What he told is what we need to hear again and again—that God loves us more than we can ever realize. Jesus gave his all to tell us this. When we look at the cross on the altar we are reminded of this great and good news.

When we eat our hot-cross buns we shall remember what this means, especially now that we've talked about it. Not only do I hope this becomes a tradition in our church, meaning it will happen next year and the year after that and so on year after year, but I hope also that you will talk to your parents about starting this tradition in your home. This morning for breakfast my family and I had hot-cross buns. We did it for a purpose—because it has meaning.

Hot-cross buns are a good reminder of what Jesus did on the cross for us in telling us about God's love.

Let us pray.
Dear God: Hot-cross buns remind us of your love, and we are thankful. Amen.

No. 11

I Gotta Be Me

Take your right hand and hold it out toward me, with the palm facing me. Now turn the palm toward you. Slowly begin to bring your hand toward your face. Closer, closer, closer yet, until you can clearly see the lines in the palm of your hand. So far so good. Keep it there. Now move your hand over slightly so that you can see your thumb. Look at the end of your thumb carefully. Do you notice all the little lines on your thumb? If you'll look at the ends of your fingers, there too you'll see a lot of little curvy ridges. What you're looking at is a thumbprint and fingerprints. Have you ever noticed them before? Sure you have. But why are they there?

I have in my brown bag this morning a big picture of a fingerprint. Here you can really see all those curvy lines or ridges. Look at it carefully, and then look again carefully at your own fingerprints. They look kind of alike, but they aren't really alike. Did you know that every one of us has his or her own special fingerprints? No two persons have fingerprints or thumbprints alike. There are now a little over four billion people in the world, and each person's fingerprints are different from everyone else's.

By the way, on your hand each finger has a different fingerprint. There is just no end to fingerprints. And did you know that the fingerprint patterns you have now will continue unchanged for as long as you live? And while I'm not going to ask you to do it now—you can do it when you get home if you want to—but if you take off your shoes and socks, you will find the same to be true concerning your toes. Yes, you have toeprints too. Nobody has toeprints like yours.

As you may have heard, the fingerprint is used to identify people. If somebody has your fingerprints, that person can find out who you are because your fingerprint is different from anyone else's. This has been done for hundreds of years. But only in recent times have we put a lot of know-how into fingerprinting so that we can better identify people. Our FBI—Federal Bureau of Investigation—has the world's largest collection of fingerprint records. The FBI uses fingerprints in its detective work, especially in its work of finding criminals. Of course, we're not criminals, but nevertheless our fingerprints always tell the truth about who we are. So when I look at mine I have to say, "I gotta be me."

I have three special thoughts about all these fingerprints. First, God is certainly a great inventor to have made all these fingerprints different. Every person who ever lived, every person living now, and every person who will live in the future has had, does have, and will have his or her own special fingerprints. Fantastic! Second, since all of us have been given our own fingerprints, I think God is trying to tell us that we're special. And third, God wants each of us to be who we are, with each of us saying, "I gotta be me."

Maybe when you go to bed tonight you can say ever so softly, "Dear God, help me to be the special person you want me to be."

Let us pray.
Dear God: Thank you for allowing each of us to be special to you. Amen.

No. 12

Hop 'Em

Once upon a time, I went to a circus. That was back when I was about your age. It was great fun. I can vividly remember it, because so few circuses came our way, and when one did, we didn't forget it—ever. Sitting under the big top with three rings of acts going on at the same time was something to see. It took some kind of looking to take it all in, and even then I couldn't see it all. And there were the clowns outside the three rings adding to the fun and entertainment. If you have been to a circus, you know all that goes on there.

One act in particular at that circus caught my eye and fancy, and I came home determined to do the same thing. It was a juggler who caused me to sit up and take special notice. Right then and there I made up my mind that I was going to learn how to juggle.

After I got home, I sat down to figure out how to do it. No one in my family could show me how to start. I had to learn on my own. If you've never tried it, believe me, it's not as easy as good jugglers make it appear. After scratching my head and pondering which hand to move first, I gave it a try. Starting off with rocks, I tried again and again by throwing them up in the air, and more than once I hit myself on the head. But that didn't stop me from trying again. I practiced and practiced, at last using rubber balls instead of rocks because they didn't hurt as much.

One doesn't learn this art of juggling overnight or in just a week. It took me many weeks before I could keep the balls in the air the right way. First, I started with one ball, trying to catch it without looking at it when it came down. Then I used two, having one in the air while I was catching and throwing the other one. And, finally, I learned to keep three going, with two in the air while catching and throwing the third one. You can imagine how proud I was when at last I did it.

I haven't juggled for a long time, except last night and early this morning. You see, I wanted to get in some practice so that I could show you that I can still do it—I think I can. My son, seeing me do this, said, "Look, Daddy is hopping them." His repeated request is, "Hop 'em, hop 'em, hop 'em, Daddy." Well, let's see if I can still juggle, or "hop 'em." I have some oranges in my bag I'll try to use.

First, with one. . .
Next, with two. . .
Now, with all three. . .
And I did it!

As are so many things in life, juggling is a simple parable about life. It tells about our knowing the right thing to do and our ability to do it. In juggling we call it coordination. In life we call it putting into action with our hands what our minds tell our hands to do. Of course, this takes practice.

How many times have we known what the right and good thing is for someone else to do, only to sit on our own hands and do nothing? Or many times we want to help, with the best of intentions, but we may do more harm than good. See what I'm talking about?

There needs to be some coordination with the good we know in our head and the good our hands can do.

Really, this is what being a Christian is all about, provided we do it with a loving heart.

Remember this: God wants to help us learn how to make our minds, our hands, and our hearts work together for what is good and right. There are some words from a hymn I love to sing that say it so well:

Take my hands and let them move
At the impulse of thy love.

Let us pray.
Dear God: May our minds, hands, and hearts work together to show love. Amen.

No. 13

More than Looks

Yesterday I got my hair cut. All you have to do is look at me to know that—that is, if you can remember what I looked like last Sunday. The barber must have thought I was crazy when I asked for some of my hair, but he gave it to me nevertheless. So, deep in my brown bag, tucked away in an envelope, are the clippings from the top of my head. See.

Question: Do you think it helped my looks to have my hair cut? I have a brother who, if he had heard me ask this question, would say nothing would help my looks. I love my brother anyway. When I arrived home from the barbershop, I asked about it, and the reply was, "He cut it a little short, but it will grow." And, of course, I didn't just get it cut to help my looks. It had been over a month since I last had it cut, and it was beginning to tickle the tops of my ears and the back of my neck. And it was also getting so long that I couldn't keep it combed.

But I haven't given you a chance to answer. Did it or didn't it help my looks? . . . .Some of you say yes, some no, and some seem to be politely saying nothing. Oh, well, that's the way it goes. If my mother were here, she would say it helped—at least, I think she would.

Wait a minute. Why am I carrying on like this? Sure, looks are important, but they aren't that important, are they? Oh, many people think they are, and they will do almost anything to improve their looks. Often it does make them more attractive. But I think people sometimes put too much emphasis on looking nice when in truth they aren't very nice people.

Another question: Which is more important, looking nice or being a nice person? It's wonderful when a person is both. Let me hurriedly say that to be nice a person doesn't have to look ugly. There is really no connection between the two. But it is too bad when we make looking pretty and beautiful so very important that we in turn forget about how people see us, whether we're grumpy and mean or happy and kind.

I will have to agree with my brother: nothing I do, be it getting a haircut or being fitted for new glasses or having my freckles removed, will help my looks. I know this. And I used to worry about it. But not anymore. The reason I don't worry is because I know God cares far more what we *are* like than what we *look* like. In fact, if we were to take all of Jesus' teachings about God, this truth would be at the top of the list.

Paul, a man who lived when Jesus lived and for a number of years after Jesus died, followed up on Jesus' teaching, pointing out what we should be like, that we should be loving, peaceful, patient, kind, good, faithful, gentle, and self-controlled. And then he said, "Let us have no self-conceit, . . . no envy of one another."

I take this all to mean that what we *are* like is more important than what we *look* like. Surely that is the way God sees us.

Let us pray.
Dear God: Thank you for being more concerned about the beauty of our lives than about the beauty of our faces, and help us to look at others the same way. Amen.

No. 14

A Love Story as Told by Peanuts

The past couple of weeks have been rough at our house. We've had our share of sickness. It was the flu. They say it's going around.

First, Tap came down with it, and then Suzanne. Tap is OK now, but his sister still has a touch of it, plus a few side effects. In a day or two she'll be better. Both children have received plenty of tender loving care.

While they were sick, our neighbor brought them each a present. In Tap's package were some peanuts. These peanuts were neither roasted nor salted. They were for planting.

And plant them we did. With the peanuts came instructions on how to plant and care for them. In just an ordinary cup we planted them as instructed, and inside that cup we put some special plant food to start them growing.

Would you like to see what has happened to these peanuts? In my bag I have the results. Have you ever seen peanuts grow? This is my first experience with peanut plants. I've been amazed at how much they have grown in this short time. All Tap did was add water to the plant food which was provided in the package with the peanuts. But he did more than that. He did this with love, with tender loving care. And they've been growing like mad! In a few days he will put each peanut plant into its own pot so that each will have more room to grow bigger.

I've done more watching than helping, for after all it was his gift and not mine. But as I watched, I was struck by the fact that this is really a love story.

The first part of this love story tells of God making these peanuts just for the love of making peanuts. That's the same reason God made you and me—for the love of it.

The second part of this love story is the tender loving care God requires us to give to these peanuts if they are to grow properly. That's what God wants us to do for others in helping them to grow up as they should. We must do it with tender loving care.

Finally, there comes that time when these peanuts will produce more peanuts. Tap will be an extremely happy boy when that happens. But if he keeps them only for himself, his happiness will not be all that it should be. It is important for him to learn to share his happiness—to share these peanuts when they are harvested. The same is true of the way we live. We must learn to share lovingly with others the good things God has allowed us to have in the first place.

All this from a peanut? Where does life come from?—from a loving God. How are we to handle life?—with tender loving care. What are we to do with the good things life provides?—lovingly share them with others.

Let us pray.
Dear God: From such a little plant, we have learned much about you and what you expect from us. Amen.

No. 15

Over and Over Again

There are many wonderful things happening in our country, and I want to tell you about two in particular.

How many of you have seen this symbol? It's three arrows chasing each other in a circle. Only in the last few years have I begun to notice it. Usually when I bring my bag on Sunday morning, I have in it what I am going to talk about. Well, this morning it's not *in* my bag; it's *on* my bag. Take a look. Notice the words beside this symbol: "recycled—recyclable." Do you know what that means?

The word cycle tells us most about what this word recycled means. Of course, a cycle goes in a circle. Your tricycles and bicycles have that word as part of their names because the wheels go around. Now, are you wondering how this bag is going to go around in circles? Don't worry, it won't. What is meant is that this bag was once before another bag or paper item, and after it was first used, it wasn't just thrown away or burned up, like we so often do with wastepaper, but it was made over again into new paper items; and that's where this bag came from. Because the paper in the bag

41

can be used over and over again, we use the symbol of a circle of three arrows, each pointing at the one ahead of it.

I think this is great. There are other things besides paper that can be recycled, and if we will do this we can save our natural resources, which just might run out if we aren't careful.

As I think about this word recycled, it causes me to wonder if people ought to be recycled too. Now what do you think of that idea? No, this doesn't mean going in circles. We do enough of that by running around every day and not getting as much done as we should. Rather, it means that God can use us over and over again, all in one lifetime too. Sometimes people feel like saying, "I'm no good anymore." But God says, "Yes, you are!"

Oh, God doesn't want our lives thrown away when we've done bad things or when it seems that we aren't needed anymore in this world. By forgiving us God makes us new again to be used again. Yes, people are recyclable too.

So try to remember: God wants us to use wisely the things of this world, and to use them over and over again if possible. And God wants us to be used over and over again in doing good as long as we live.

Let us pray.
Dear God: Make us new again. Amen.

No. 16

As Good as New

I'm sure you know by heart the verse I'm going to say.
Most likely your mother or father taught it to you.

> Humpty Dumpty sat on a wall,
> Humpty Dumpty had a great fall;
> All the king's horses, and all the king's men
> Couldn't put Humpty together again.

Why don't we all say it together? Here we go.

> Humpty Dumpty sat on a wall,
> Humpty Dumpty had a great fall;
> All the king's horses, and all the king's men
> Couldn't put Humpty together again.

This morning I've brought in my brown bag a picture of
Humpty Dumpty. Take a look. Wild, isn't it? It's kind of
modern. It's so modern, in fact, that maybe it deserves
the second verse someone wrote:

> But an American doctor,
> With patience and glue,
> Put Humpty together again
> As good as new.

There is a lesson to be
learned here. Aside from being a
good egg, Humpty Dumpty was
just like any other egg—breakable.
And that would be the end of poor
Humpty Dumpty if not put together
again.

We can say that when a person dies it's kind of like a dropped egg. No matter how good a person is, someday his or her life will be broken in death. The life on this earth will break apart. We will not live forever on this earth. Once we have died and our life on earth is broken apart, nobody can bring us back to live in this world again. Not even an American doctor can put us back together again. But there is something else to say. There is another verse we can add to our story. Listen to this:

> But a wonderful God,
> Using love as glue,
> Can put us together again
> As good as new.

Yes, God loves us while we live in this world. That we know! And God will continue to love us even after we die. That we must also know! When we die, our God does a very loving thing for us, giving us a new kind of life—life everlasting. We don't know exactly what it's like—yet—except that it's going to be wonderful.

This is Easter Sunday, and it's good we can talk together about this. Easter really tells us that after our life on earth is broken apart—after we die—there is another life that will be very beautiful.

If this new life could be given to Humpty Dumpty, we'd have to call Humpty an Easter egg, wouldn't we? But the story is really about us. After we die God wants to put us together again in a new life. Through Jesus Christ God has told us this. It makes us Easter people.

Let us pray.

Dear God: Thank you for being so good to us, in this life and in the life to come. Amen.

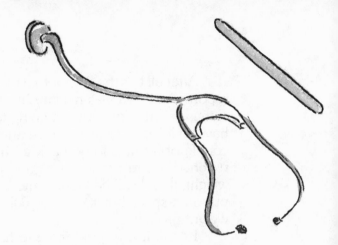

No. 17

Checkup

If you'll excuse me for just a moment, I have something to do.

[A tongue depressor and a stethoscope are taken from the brown bag and used in a mock physical examination.]

Are you wondering what I'm doing? I'm doing just what the doctor did this past week. Oh, perhaps I should tell you what happened to me when I went to the doctor's office.

I went for one reason, to find out whether or not I was healthy. It had been some time since my last physical examination. All was OK then, and since then I've felt fine—no pains or hurts. But one may feel as if nothing is wrong when in fact something is wrong, and if it's detected early enough, very often it can be corrected. That was my main reason for having a physical exam. I wanted to know if anything was wrong.

Well, this doctor put me through a lot of tests. With a tongue depressor my throat was checked. With a stethoscope like this, my heart beat was checked for its regularity and sound. Then a machine was used to sound out my heart in a more detailed way, and it is called an electrocardiograph. The nurse stuck my finger in order to get blood that could be tested. I was weighed. The doctor looked in my ears and eyes. I was given almost every kind of test, some I've mentioned and some I would prefer not to mention. And on top of this, I was asked what seemed like hundreds of questions about how I felt and about my past medical history.

After all this the doctor told me about my health. The report was that I was healthy but that I needed to lose some weight. Now I'm not going to tell you how much I have to lose. However, I have another appointment in a couple of months to go back to the doctor and get weighed. If I'm not making good progress in losing weight, then I will be "regimented" or, in other words, be put on a special diet. But enough of this talk about my weight problem.

I think it is a good thing to have a physical examination at least once a year. For you see, it is important to know the truth about our health.

And as I lay on the table during the examination, I couldn't help but think that that was where I really belonged. By this I mean it is good to have this type of examination. The reason is that God wants us to take good care of our bodies. The Bible says, "your body is a temple. . .which you have from God. . . .So glorify God in your body." Thus, it is important that we eat good food, exercise correctly, and allow the doctor to check on our health. That's why I had a checkup and why in the days to come I'll be doing what the doctor told me to do, as well as what God wants me to do about taking good care of my body.

Let us pray.

Dear God: Remind us again and again to take good care of our bodies. Amen.

No. 18

Forever Building

Did you ever decide to do something, only to be told by your father or mother that before you start you had better sit down with a pencil and paper to plan out your idea in detail?

When I was told to do this by my parents, my reaction was always, "Why?" When I was your age, I was one who always wanted to rush at once into my project without a lot of planning. Looking back on those times when I did as my parents requested and on those times when I didn't, I now know why they wanted me to plan ahead.

The reason is this: I had more success in what I did if I first sat down and carefully planned it out. Makes sense, doesn't it?

Building this church required careful planning. Now that it is finished, we can tell that a great deal of careful planning went into its design. It's beautiful! But think how ugly it might have been if we had tried to build it without any plans. That's a horrible thought!

I've brought with me this morning a set of the plans used to build our church. And, of course, it's in my brown bag. It's called a blueprint—I guess because it's printed on blue paper. Here, take a look. There it is, our church in every detail. Look at a certain part of the church, like those beams, or that flower box, or those doors, or this altar; they are all here in the plans. All of this was thought out even before the workers started to build. Who thought this out and put it on paper? A group in our church, the building committee, worked long and hard with an architect, a person who designs buildings. Together they spent many hours, days, weeks, and months planning this church. After the worship service this morning, I will be glad to show you what these blueprints look like close up.

God requires us to do some planning about the way we live, wanting us to decide what kind of persons we want to become. Think how unorganized and confused life would be for us if we didn't do some planning. Here are some of the things God wants us to build into our lives: respect for the feelings of others; kindness at all times; honesty in every situation; patience when needed; helpfulness to those who need our assistance; love that never ends; faith in God; loyalty to Jesus. Yes, these are some of the materials necessary for building the kind of life God wants us to build.

Now we aren't going to get the job done right by just wishing it were done. We must take this plan of living and start working on it.

Do you know how the plan for this church differs from our plan for right living? We have finished with this church building, but with our personal lives we are never finished. We are forever building on the kind of life God wants us to have.

Let us pray.
Dear God: Help us to plan our lives well. Amen.

No. 19

Hand in Glove

I didn't want to do it, but I knew I had to. It was that time of year, with spring just a few days away. So last Monday I went out into the yard with rake and shovel in hand.

And it was just plain hard work! Raking all the dead grass out of the lawn and then turning the soil for a garden plot caused me to huff and puff. I also got a few blisters doing all that work. However, if it hadn't been for my gloves, I would have gotten more blisters. I've brought them along in my brown bag. Let me put them on.

There. How about that? Is this the first time you've see red work gloves? Of course, color has nothing to do with how well they protect my hands while working. It's not their appearance that matters, but it's the protection they give my hands. These are good gloves.

However, after I put them on, do you know what I wanted to do? Take them off! These gloves are used for hard work and, more times than not when it comes to hard work, I'd rather rest and take it easy. Most people feel that way about work.

But last Monday I kept them on and did what I had to do. It wasn't really as bad as I thought it was going to be. Once I had put these gloves on and got started and kept at it, I began to enjoy what I was doing. The dread and reluctance went out of the job and I was happy to be doing what I had been putting off. In fact, a sense of satisfaction came over me, and when I was through I felt it was a job well done.

And then that night and much of the next day a gentle rain fell, making me doubly happy that my yard and garden plot were ready.

Two thoughts came to mind about this. One, which came while I was working, was that we often put off the work we should be doing. In like manner, the good we should do, we often neglect. For example, we should rake out the dead grass of bitterness, hate, jealousy, cruel words, and so on, so that the living grass of goodwill and love can green up quickly for the betterment of all. But in order for this to happen, we must put on the gloves of determination and keep them on until the work is done.

And the second thought was about the rain. It was a blessing from heaven, with God taking part in making my yard and garden grow. In like manner, when we help others, God will send down a gentle blessing, giving life and growth to our good deeds. Let's always do our work well, and God will bless our work as well as our deeds of goodwill.

Let us pray.
Dear God: Keep us from putting off doing good. Amen.

No. 20

All Decked Out

What do you think I have in my bag this morning? It's something my grandparents would never have brought to church, nor would they ever have had it at home. But times have changed. No one here will be upset if out of my bag I take a deck of playing cards.

How many of you have a deck of playing cards at home? They can be a lot of fun. But I will have to confess that I really don't know how to play many different kinds of card games. I play solitaire, hearts, and a little bridge. That's about it. But when I was your age, I learned how to play a really fun game. When I first played it, I didn't think it was much fun; however, after that whenever I played it with others, I thought it was just great. Would you like to learn how to play it? Watch carefully.
[In a flipping way, the cards are sprayed out over the children.]

Now wasn't that fun? Oh, I forgot to tell you the name of this game. It's called "fifty-two pick up." The rules of the game are that I flip the cards like I did and you pick them up—all fifty-two of them.

As you are picking up these cards, I want you to pretend you are doing something else. Pretend you are picking up litter.

Many people play fifty-two pick up with their trash. They throw it down and hope someone else will pick it up. And when lots of people litter, our world looks very messy with wastepaper, cans, old tires, bottles, boxes, and many other things scattered here, there, and everywhere. It's not pretty to see.

Several years ago I went with a youth group to pick up trash along the highway. Our section was about half a mile long, and we were surprised at how much trash we collected. Would you believe we picked up two, not one but two, pickup truck loads? That's the truth! This is sad because littering is one thing people do that makes God's beautiful world look ugly and neglected.

As you pick up these cards, just imagine you are picking up litter, doing your part to keep God's world clean and beautiful.

This coming week is called Earth Week. It is a special week, a time each year when many persons not only think about a clean earth but also get out and help clean it up. Let's not forget to do our part. It's a true saying, and some of you have heard it, "Every litter bit hurts."

Let us pray.

Dear God: Help us do our part in keeping your world beautiful. Amen.

No. 21

The Best Policy

It's that time of year again. Time to plant things in the ground. Some of you have already started planting in your gardens. I have to admit that I have only turned the soil in mine. Maybe I'll get around to doing some work in it this coming week.

I know one thing for sure. I have some things I need to plant and soon—geraniums. Last fall when it was time for frost, I dug up all the geraniums in front of our house, put them in milk cartons that had been cut down, and stored them in the basement for the winter. I had about fifteen in all and about ten survived. Now I must replant them.

But I must plant even more geraniums than these. At the beginning of last week, I noted that the hardware store (of all places) was selling geraniums for nineteen cents a plant. Well, I stopped by to take a look at them. Did they have the geraniums! Hundreds of them. After looking them over (they were outside the store), I went in to tell the cashier that I wanted twenty-five plants. I paid for them and then went back out to select the ones I wanted.

Here in my brown bag is one of the geranium plants. I brought it to show you what it looks like. They're beautiful plants when they bloom—with red flowers.

As I was making my selections, a bad thought entered my mind. Why not take more than twenty-five? No one would know the difference. I could do it rather easily. My car was parked close by. All I had to do was open the trunk and put in more plants than I had paid for. No one was standing there checking how many I took.

53

That was a very tempting thought!

Do you know what I said to myself? "No!" That's what I said. Granted, the store owner may not have known, that is until all the plants had been sold and some counting had been done. Who would have known I had done it? However, as far as I was concerned, that wasn't the point I considered important. I would know about it, and so would God. So, that took care of that bad thought.

And even more, it just wouldn't be right or fair to the owner of the store. If I had been the owner of that store, I wouldn't want someone to steal from me. And I'm sure you would feel the same way. So again I said no to that tempting thought. Honesty is the best policy.

I came home with twenty-eight geranium plants. Yes, I bought three more before I left. That's the truth. If you want to, you may come by this summer and see how my "honest" geraniums are growing.

Let us pray.
Dear God: Keep us honest. Amen.

No. 22

It Takes Practice

Yesterday morning at 6:30 I did something I haven't done in a long time—played a game of golf. In my bag I have my scorecard. It will tell you how well I played, and I didn't play well at all. For that reason, I don't know if I really want to show it to you. It's kind of like a bad report card.

My parents are visiting us. My father brought his golf clubs in the trunk of his car. Now when my father brings his clubs over six hundred miles, I don't have to ask whether or not he wants to play golf. So we decided that early Saturday morning, before a lot of people crowded the golf course, would be the best time to play. And we were right.

After we had signed in, paid our money, and picked up the scorecard, we got ready to tee off. When I say tee off that means hit the ball. I noticed there was one person standing behind us who was also waiting to tee off. He was alone, so I asked him if he would like to play along with us. He said he would be happy to.

I soon realized what kind of golfer he was. Good! Very good! He teed off, and his ball took off like a jet. He made many, many beautiful shots while we played. Only after we had played about three holes did I see a tag on his golf bag that had the initials PGA on it, which stand for Professional Golfers' Association, and to be able to put that on your golf bag you have to be good, very good. He said in reply to my question that he wasn't a professional golfer, the kind we read about in the sports pages of the newspaper. But he is the nearest to one I've ever come.

I kept the score. That means that on the first hole I had the highest score. In golf, you don't want the highest score; you want the lowest—whoever takes the fewest strokes to put the ball in the hole is the winner. I'm not a good golfer. Several members of this church, who have played with me in the past, know the truth of that. I am what they call an occasional golfer. Yesterday, I was simply terrible. In fact, I'm going to tear up this scorecard right now so that no one will see it. I'll swear my father to secrecy, and I'll not tell you the name of that other golfer. You'll never know from me.

That other golfer was nice about my being a duffer. The word duffer means not a very good golfer. He even offered some helpful advice from time to time which I greatly appreciated. And he said these encouraging words, "You have potential." But he really put his finger on the problem when he said I need a great deal of practice if ever I am going to learn how to play golf.

I couldn't help but think how true this is in religion. Take prayer, for example. Prayer is talking to God and listening to what God has to say to us. But if we only do this two or three times a year, we're not going to know how to pray very well. And we could go down the list on so many other things we do in religion, such as read the Bible, think about the well-being of others, go to church, and so on. The same truth applies here as it does in golf: If we don't do it often, we won't do it well.

Sure, it is far more important how we respond to God and to other people than how we play golf. However, the rule of golf still applies to life: If we are to do well what we are attempting to do, we must do it often. In a religious way we often say it like this: We must practice what we preach.

Let us pray.
Dear God: Help us to practice being Christians each day. Amen.

No. 23

To Tell It Like It Is

There are many things I enjoy doing, and playing softball is one. Just talking about it brings back memories of church picnics in past years. I like remembering how we played softball for hours, each getting a turn at bat, and with all having lots of fun. I'm eagerly awaiting this year's picnic for this very reason, as well as for that good food and the great fellowship we all have together. And do you realize that the church picnic is just two weeks away? After we have eaten and talked, let it be heard by all, "Play ball!" And here in my bag is the softball we'll play with when that time comes.

For me, the enjoyment of playing softball goes back to my school days. I've always enjoyed it—except once. That once brings up a very embar-rassing incident, one I would prefer you not mention outside of this sanctuary. It happened when I was in junior high school. Along with a few other good players, we were the Babe Ruths and Hank Aarons of the playground. We were the home-run hitters. Everyone looked up to us, or at least we liked to think they did.

My team was up at bat. We had runners on the bases. Since it wasn't my turn to bat, I decided I would help out by being a third-base coach. The next batter hit an infield ball, one very hard to handle. Our runner on second hesitated, questioning whether or not he should try for third base. I waved the runner on. Here came the ball. The third baseman missed the ball, and it rolled on past the base. And here's where I made my goof. In the excitement, with my runner going for home plate, I picked up the ball and winged it home. If I say so myself, it was a beautiful throw, right to the catcher. Do you get the picture?

What had I done? I had thrown out my own player. Were my team members angry! And what did I do about it? I tried to justify what I had just done, saying, "Their third baseman needed help." Help? The facts being what they were, I had to admit I had really goofed.

Isn't it strange how we often try to justify our wrongs, even when the wrongs are so plain? Why do we do this? To save face is one reason. To make ourselves acceptable to ourselves is another reason. And who among us hasn't done this? Yes, we all have. Often we want to justify our actions even to the point of being slightly untruthful. Sure, we may partly succeed in making ourselves look a little better than we really are, but then a part of us always knows the truth.

The truth God wants us to live with is this: tell it like it is. That's not always an easy thing to do. It sometimes hurts our pride. At times when we have to tell it like it is we may be somewhat sad. But when all is said and done, the truth is what makes life happier for us and others. It's a lesson to learn early and to not forget.

Let us pray.
Dear God: Help us to have the courage to always tell it like it is. Amen.

No. 24

A Nugget of Truth

I did it. Yes, I did something I've wanted to do for a long time. I went down into a gold mine.

That's right, a gold mine. My family and I went up to Cripple Creek, which is less than an hour's drive from Colorado Springs. And while we were there we went down deep into the earth to see where they get that yellow metal from which they make things like rings and other kinds of jewelry.

After we had paid our admission to see the mine, we climbed into an old elevator that took us deep, deep down inside the mountain. This particular mine went down about thirteen hundred feet. We stopped on the third level, although there were seven levels, or floors, underneath us. In that deep, damp, rock-walled tunnel we saw where they mined the gold. The guide explained it all very well. And I caught my imagination running away with me, seeing myself as a gold miner with pick and shovel in hand. It was very exciting until I realized what hard work it was chiseling the gold ore out of the hard stone. Then I let my imagination rest and went on with the guided tour. Really, it was a lot of fun, and I learned much about gold-mining.

When we came back up to the surface (oh, it was good to see the light of day again!), they had a bucket of gold ore from which we could take souvenirs. The guide said it was neither high-grade nor low-grade ore, just medium-grade. That means it wasn't the best, and it wasn't the worst, just so-so. But if we had enough of it and knew how to get it out, we could get gold out of those

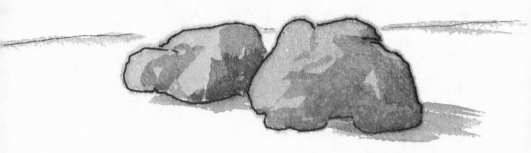

rocks. In my brown bag I have some gold-ore rocks for you to see and have.

There was a sign in the gold-mine office that caught my eye. It came from the Bible:

> The judgments of the Lord are true and righteous altogether.
> More to be desired are they than gold, yea, than much fine gold.

What does that mean? There is more than one answer, but here is what I think it means.

Those miners who worked the mine long ago thought that if they just found gold and more gold they would have it made. All would be well for them. What else would they need? They worked hard for this. But the sign says to me that gold is not the only thing that makes a person happy. The good life and true happiness are found elsewhere.

Real happiness is found in our hearts, not in a stone. It's not a metal like my ring; it's acts of love and kindness to others. At times this may be difficult, but believe me, we will then have something more valuable than gold, "yea, than much fine gold." That is what is really important to God. And what is important to God should and must be important to us.

Let us pray.

Dear God: Help us find true happiness, the kind that makes life good and gives it meaning and worth. Amen.

No. 25

High-grading/Low-grading

Last week some of you heard me talk about going down into a gold mine. While I was down there, I learned something about the men who worked in the mines in those early gold-mining days. What those gold miners did was take gold-filled ore rocks home with them when they quit work in the evening. It was called high-grading. Now the only problem with high-grading was that the gold ore wasn't theirs to take. This is how they did it.

One way was to put it in their lunch pails. In time the people in charge of the mines became wise to what was happening, and so they began to check the lunch pails when the workers went home—which put a stop to that!

Then the workers began putting the ore rocks in their pockets. But once again the front office became wise, and they ordered them to wear clothes furnished by the mining company. When they arrived at work in the morning, they had to change into those clothes, and when they went home at night, they changed again into their own clothes.

Once again, the miners tried another way of high-grading. When digging out the gold, they found a lot of ore dust that had gold in it. I've brought some of this dust in my bag so you can see what it looks like. I didn't high-grade it; they let me take it. Because the mines were damp and cool, it was only natural that the miners would wear long underwear. They used the underwear to their advantage. While no one was looking, or at least when the boss wasn't around, they would rub this dust into their long underwear. Here, let me show you how they

61

did it. In my bag I also have some long underwear. See. All they did was rub it in like this. Then, when they arrived home, they would carefully wash it, save the water, let the ore dust settle to the bottom of the tub, dry it out, and take out the gold.

Why did they do this? They thought they had a good reason. Their pay for mining the gold was not high; often they had just barely enough to put food on the table, clothes on their backs, and a roof overhead. By high-grading they could make up to ten extra dollars a day on the average. That was big money back then. Another excuse for doing this was that everyone did it—and most everyone did. It's said that high-grading not only paid for the extras in life but also was put in the offering plates at church on Sunday.

But was it the right thing to do? No! No matter how many excuses they had, taking what didn't belong to them was stealing, and we all know that this is wrong. I've heard it said that stealing is a low-down thing to do. We might want to call this low-grading.

We today aren't tempted to high-grade/low-grade as they did, but we are at times tempted to take from another what isn't ours. It may be a piece of bubble gum in a store or a toy from a friend or money we see lying somewhere belonging to someone else. We may think we have a good excuse for taking it, and we may devise a smart way of taking it and not get caught. But it isn't right to do. You know it, and I know it too. In fact, God has made it very clear that this isn't what we're supposed to do, saying, "Thou shalt not steal." And when we steal, God knows about it as soon as we do it.

Yes, the temptation to take what isn't ours is often very strong. But we must resist and take not. God wants us to resist. In the long run we'll be happier.

Let us pray.

Dear God: Help us never to take what doesn't belong to us. Amen.

No. 26

All the Animals

"Let's go to the zoo," someone shouted. And I said to my family, "Great idea!" So we went to the zoo and had a wonderful time.

How many of you have been to the zoo? Good. Then you know what we saw. The first animal was the rhinoceros. That's one animal I wouldn't want to meet outside the zoo. It could hurt a person with that big, hairy horn on its nose and with its tanklike charge. Then we saw many different kinds of antelope from Africa and Asia, ones with long, curvy horns. Beautiful! We saw zebras. You know what a zebra looks like, don't you? And a zoo wouldn't be a zoo without elephants. Were they big! Wow! Those giraffes were big too, especially their long necks. After that, we saw the bears, the lions, the tigers, and other kinds of wild cats, the hippopotamus, the rare birds, the reptiles, the anteaters, the penguins, the monkeys, plus many other animals I don't have time to tell you about.

There was one animal in particular that I liked, and I just have to mention it. It's called an orangutan. How best can I describe it? Let me just show you one. No, I don't have a real live one in my brown bag, but I did bring a picture of one to show you. There. Strange-looking isn't it? It reminds me of a funny thing that happened to me.

Some years ago when I was looking at the orangutans in another zoo, a cousin of mine whom I hadn't seen for a long time came up behind me and said, "What are you doing, looking at yourself?" Now I ask you, does this look like me? I said, "Be careful what you say; you're related to me."

All in all, the zoo is a fun place.

When I was walking around looking at all those animals, two thoughts kept coming to mind. First, God certainly has a wonderful imagination, creating so many different kinds of animals, from the long snakes to the big hippopotamus to the tiny monkey. God even made us. All these animals are so very different and yet all are so wonderful in the place where God puts them.

My other thought was that God has given us human animals a special task, that of being responsible for all the other animals, even those that will harm us or those that we think are ugly. God has given us minds that are able to know what is the best for the other animals. It's sad to say, but we haven't always used our abilities to think the way God want us to. We have not cared for many of the animals as we should. Some animals have all been killed off and others nearly so. That's sad. The zoos of our world, along with a good many people not connected with the zoos, are helping some kinds of animals to make a comeback.

We must think of all the animals as God does. "And God said, 'Let the earth bring forth living creatures according to their kinds.'. . . And it was so. . . .And God saw that it was good."

Let us pray.

Dear God: We want to do our part in taking care of your animals. Amen.

No. 27

Freedom—At the End of the Nose

A re you ready to celebrate? It will soon be the day
when we celebrate the independence of our country,
remembering when we as a people declared that we were
a nation separate from England. We usually celebrate it
with fireworks, picnics, and speeches about the past,
present, and future greatness of our country. You know
what it is, don't you? Sure, it's the Fourth of July.

In my brown bag I have "Fourth of July" written on
a piece of paper in red, white, and blue. I have written just
below it another word: FREEDOM. Many people would
agree that these words go together, but let me tell you
why I can't think of the Fourth of July without thinking of
freedom.

It goes back to when I was young. There was a man,
a close family friend, who lived in my home town. He told
a story I've never forgotten. I heard him tell it many times.
Here is his story.

Once there was a man who heard about our free
country. He lived in a country in Europe where freedom
was extremely limited. He managed to escape and make
his way by boat to this country. As he stepped off the
boat, he took a deep breath and then walked up to a
person standing nearby. This person, seeing the
newcomer coming toward him, extended a hand of
welcome. Instead of shaking hands, which was the polite
thing to do, this new arrival doubled up his fist and hit this
man in the nose.

"Why did you do that?" asked the man who was hit.

"This is a free country, isn't it? I can do what I want
to do."

The man who had been hit replied, "This may be a free country, but your freedom stops where my nose begins."

That story makes me think about freedom, especially at this time of year. My friend always told the same story on the Fourth of July. The early founders of our country who wrote the Declaration of Independence and the man who was hit in the nose said about the same thing, and it was this: We have freedom to do what we wish, but when that freedom interferes with the rights of someone else, we're in the wrong.

Perhaps you've heard what those early founders felt to be extremely important when they were declaring our country's independence, but it's worth hearing again: "We hold these truths to be self-evident: that all men are created equal, that they are endowed by their Creator with certain unalienable rights; that among these are life, liberty, and the pursuit of happiness." Of course, we should know that when they said "all men" they really meant "all people."

Well, that's talking about freedom using fancy language and some big words, but that's what we'll be celebrating this Fourth of July. It's a God-given freedom to do as we please. But we can't please God and do as Jesus taught unless we use our freedom in a responsible way, with love causing us to stop short of punching someone in the nose.

Thus, love and freedom go together. I've written this word LOVE right next to FREEDOM. And we know the reason.

Let us pray.
Dear God: Help us to remember what our freedom means and how we are to use it. Amen.

No. 28

Work to Do

"Has Dad gone yet?" I used to say this to my twin brother. We weren't much older at that time than you are now. Let me explain.

I grew up on a farm. As some of your dads and moms can tell you, there is always some job yet to be done on the farm. For example, the cows have to be milked, the pigs fed, the barn cleaned out, the water tank filled, the fence fixed, the eggs gathered, and as if all this weren't enough, the weeds cut along the front fence. These are just a few jobs I remember being asked to do. No, they didn't all have to be done at the same time. But to the best of my memory it seemed that by the time we had finished a job it was time to do it again. So goes life on the farm.

When it came to work, my brother and I were kind of like Tom Sawyer and Huck Finn; we avoided it like the plague. We would rather go ride horses or hunt for arrowheads or fool around with what I have in my brown bag—a pole, a line, and a hook. Many times Dad would want to know where we were, only to have Mom say, "Look down at the creek; they're probably fishing."

My dad had an eight-to-five job in town, and although he did his fair share—no, more than his fair share—of the work on the farm early and late in the day, there was still more than enough for us to do. It wasn't just do this and then do that; rather, he always thought of at least ten jobs, if not more. So, on a sky-high, beautiful summer day, you can imagine how this would ruin the best-laid plans of two boys. He expected us to get the work done, and that was that! My brother and I would sometimes hide out until he was gone in order to keep him from thinking of even more things to do. Already he had left enough instructions for us with Mom. Looking back, I feel sure that our absences did get us out of some work, but by no means all of it.

But also, looking back on those boyhood days, I am not too proud of myself. Dad needed our help. And what were we doing? We were looking for ways to get out of work.

I'm wiser now, although I still try to avoid some of the work I know I should be doing. That is what we all do some of the time, right? And we know better too. Now I am called upon by God to do many things. Part of me wants to lay low and let someone else do it. But that won't do. God knows what I am doing as well as what I am not doing. I need to get with it.

For you too this has meaning. Each and every day there are things God wants you to do, like show kindness to someone who has been hurt, help your mother and dad, say your prayers, . . .the list goes on.

To be sure, there is a time to go fishing. But we shouldn't do this all the time. When there is work to do, we need to put the old fishing pole back where we found it and get on with what we must do. This is what Jesus taught about God, that God is still at work in the world, and that we all have work to do.

Let us pray.
Dear God: Forgive us for trying to run away from the work we know we should be doing. Amen.

No. 29

Keep It Natural

I would like to have your opinion on something I just happen to have in my brown bag—two rocks.

Which of these two rocks is more pleasing to the eye? This one has written on it "Jim + Mary." The other doesn't have anything written on it. Which one do you like better? Some of you seem to be saying that this one with Jim + Mary is your choice, and others are saying that this rock without any writing on it is your choice. Both are right.

I know that none of you wrote "Jim + Mary" on the rock because I wrote it, but let's pretend that one of you did write it. If by chance you were the one who wrote "Jim + Mary" on the small rock, it would be beautiful to you because it has a special meaning for you. It means you love the other person because the plus sign means love. And that is a beautiful thing to write. It could also be pretty to you because of the beautiful colors used in writing on this rock.

But in another sense, in another place, this writing wouldn't be pretty at all, at least not to me. I saw it written on a big rock. Do you know where I saw it? On a beautiful rock cliff up in the mountains. There it was, Jim + Mary. I thought it was ugly.

Now, there is a big difference between this little rock which I have in my hand and those rocks out there in their natural setting. This little one is mine, but those out there belong to us all. To write Jim + Mary on this small rock is fine, but to write the same thing on those rocks out there is wrong.

It is wrong because it ruins the beauty of nature, the beauty God created. It makes me sad to see something like this. Believe me, I saw a lot of other things scribbled on rocks and carved on trees. Not only does it make me sad, but it also makes me mad. I think it makes God feel the same way.

Whenever my son sees this kind of thing, he says, "Keep it natural." He's right! That's the right thing to do. So remember this whenever you go out into God's beautiful world, whether it's up in the mountains or down in the valleys or out on the prairie: Keep it natural.

Let us pray.

Dear God: You've made a beautiful world, and we want to help keep it that way. Amen.

No. 30

A Home in Gloryland

It's a good morning even though it's a sad morning.
As you heard me say just a few minutes ago, our
friend Dean K———was killed yesterday. I feel it is my
place to talk with you about this sad fact. I learned about
it last night, and while I was planning to talk with you
about another matter this morning, I will talk about the
accident instead. The other can wait.

You know Dean because he has been teaching you
to sing in church school. With his guitar he helped you
sing songs like "Do, Lord," "Put Your Hand in the
Hand," "I'm Gonna Sing," and many others. In my
brown bag I have the kind of songbook Dean used when
he sang with you. Here it is. Yes, he made singing fun!

Dean has also played his guitar and sung for us
during the worship service. In fact, just a few weeks ago
he sang and played in a very moving way "Amazing
Grace." And just last week I talked to him about the
possibility of your singing in the worship service some of
those songs you've learned. He thought it would be
something you would like to do. In spite of what has
happened, I hope you will still do this, remembering as
you do it how good it was of Dean to teach you these
songs of faith.

I said the word friend when I mentioned Dean's
name to you a few moments ago. And in truth he was a
friend to many people. Often I've asked him to help me,
and as a good friend he did. When he died, he was
helping a friend find her dogs. They had been stolen and,
being a pilot, Dean was trying to locate them from the air.

71

The plane crashed. He died helping another person in need. That is just the way he was—always concerned about others. We who knew Dean well will long remember him as a friend who wanted to help others.

But Dean didn't want to die, nor did God want him to die. Something went wrong. God is just as sad about Dean's death as we are, for Dean was still a young man, only twenty-four years old, with many more years of life to live. But the accident happened, and not only are we sad, but so is God.

However, God doesn't let it all end in sadness. While in the days, weeks, and years ahead there will be sadness on our part whenever we think about Dean, still God is right now doing something that isn't sad. God is talking with Dean face-to-face. In other words, Dean is with God. We who knew him well know that this is true.

While this is a sad morning, it is also a good morning, for life goes on for us. And all is well for Dean for he is in the presence of God. I imagine that right now Dean is singing the first stanza of "Do, Lord," which goes like this, "I've got a home in gloryland that outshines the sun." Dean is in heaven.

Let us pray.
Dear God: Let us not forget that Dean is with you. Amen.

No. 31

Who Gets the Biggest Piece?

"You got more than I did!" "No, I didn't!" "Yes, you did." That's what my brother and I used to say to each other when we had only one candy bar and had to divide it between us. If he did the dividing, I wasn't satisfied, and if I did it, he wasn't satisfied. Something had to give, and neither of us was willing to give the other more than he kept for himself. We often argued over just such a simple thing.

How many of you have experienced this kind of problem?

My mother solved the problem for us. I can't remember when she first did it, but no doubt she stepped between us with this solution because she was tired of hearing us argue. This was her solution, and I must say that it was very, very simple. Rather than explaining it in so many words, let me demonstrate her solution with two volunteers—Margaret and Tim.

I have a candy bar in my bag. It has to be divided between you two. Margaret, I want you to cut it in half. Now, before you divide it, I want you to know that you're not going to get first choice. Tim is. So, it becomes important to you—that is, if you want your fair share—to cut this candy bar just right. Go ahead. Now, Tim, you choose. Margaret, if Tim had gotten a larger piece than you, it would have been your fault or your decision, and you wouldn't have any cause to complain or argue about it. Right?

73

That's the way my mother solved the problem of dividing a candy bar between the two of us. It always worked.

While it always worked, and many times it was the *only* way to solve this kind of problem, there is yet another problem in doing it this way.

By making sure you cut it just right, so that the other doesn't get a bigger piece, it really causes you to think more about yourself than about the other person. In short, it makes you a bit selfish. This can be a very big problem.

There is no easy answer to this problem, mainly because it is so natural to look out for one's self-interest. There is a time and place for doing this, whether it is just in cutting a candy bar or in the bigger decisions of life. But since we are Christians, it is important that we not be so selfish and be more concerned about the other person.

This is what Jesus taught his followers to do. He taught that we should have a concern that goes beyond just ourselves. We do this with love in our hearts. He said, "This is my commandment, that you love one another as I have loved you."

This means that we should not always insist on getting a larger piece of the candy bar or whatever else has to be divided. We must be controlled with a love that is willing to give more than we get.

I have another candy bar in my bag, a large one. I can cut it up into enough pieces so we can all share it. And I'll even give you permission to eat it now—right here. But remember, if the person next to you gets a little bigger piece than you do, don't complain. Just be happy for that other person.

Let us pray.

Dear God: We want to share with others in a way that is fair. Amen.

No. 32

The Flower Test

I love flowers. Beautiful is the word we most often use to describe them. Not only do they come in all shapes and colors, but we also use them for many purposes, from adding a wonderful thought to our worship service to giving them to those we love.

Have you ever given flowers to someone you love? Or have you ever used a flower to tell if someone loves you? I've done both many times. Here, let me show you how to use a flower to tell if someone loves you.

It's best to use a wild flower for this test, like this black-eyed Susan I picked on the way to church and now have in my bag. Out it comes. And here's how you do it. You hold the flower by the stem and pull off the petals one at a time, saying as you do it, "She loves me; she loves me not; she loves me; she loves me not; she loves me; she loves me not." Of course, you can use the word he instead of she. With each petal you alternate yes and no, and you continue this until all the petals are pulled off. When you pull off the last petal, the yes or no will tell you whether or not the person loves you.

I did this a lot when I was your age. Maybe you've done this too. I think I'll see if it still works. Now I'm thinking of a very special person—my wife. Let's see if she loves me.

. . . .   Ah, she does!

Well, even if the flower would have told me no, I know that she does, because she told me so this morning.

If you decide to use the flower test to know if the person you want to love you really does, let me warn you

75

that this test is not always reliable. Even if it comes out the opposite of your wish, it's best not to take this too seriously. Rather, check it out some other way which is more reliable. Anyway, it's all a great deal of fun.

If we want to know whether or not God loves us, we don't have to go through the flower test. Already we know. How? God has told us through Jesus, the Bible, ministers, parents, and our friends. And it is a wonderful thing to know.

Unfortunately, some people want to doubt God's love. They want to pull it apart to see if it is real. And often even then they aren't certain of the answer. But we don't have to doubt God's love for us. Remember this:

God loves us!

God loves each one of us!

God loves us now and forever!

Why have we come here this morning? To remind ourselves of this wonderful love. But we have also come for another reason—to say to God, as Jesus has taught us to say, "We love you!" That is why we have flowers on the altar this morning. They aren't there just to be beautiful for us; they are our way of saying to God, "We love you!" This too is a flower test; however, it's much more reliable than the other kind.

Let us pray.

Dear God: We love you and we're happy you love us. Amen.

No. 33

That's My Name

What happens when someone calls your name? Henry! Elizabeth! Tommy! Sara! If you're like me, you perk up your ears and listen very hard. There may be a lot of noise going on at the time, like a radio playing in the background or other people talking, but amidst all this, if someone says your name, you notice it.

This happened to me last night. There I was hard at work on my sermon. The typewriter was going clickity-click, clickity-click, clickity-click. In the background the radio was broadcasting a baseball game and my favorite team was losing. Both our children were making their share of noise too. It was their bedtime and they weren't quite ready to go to bed. Our son had talked his mother into reading to him before being tucked in. All this was going on while I was working on that sermon. Then I heard it. Mother was reading from *Dr. Seuss's A B C*. When she came to the J, she read it. I've put Dr. Seuss's book in my bag and brought it to read to you.

BIG J
 little j
What begins with j?
 Jerry Jordan's
 jelly jar
 and jam
 begin that way.

Jerry Jordan—that's me! As soon as my son heard this, he just had to come over and show me the page with my name on it.

Everybody has a name. That's important. You have a name, and that's important to me. If I know your name and someone says it, then I know who they are talking about. You. But not only does a name tell who you are, it also says something even more important, that you are a special person. This is what your name says to me. For the people back in the Bible, that was what a name was all about. It told others who a person was and of that person's importance.

But we have a problem with names, don't we? This is especially so when we meet a lot of people. We tend to forget what their names are. And how do we solve this problem? We can begin by wanting to remember the name. It helps if we use as often as we can the new name we have learned. Then we must take a special interest in that person. It is important that we make an extra effort to get to know the persons we meet. We want them to do this for us, so let's do the same for them. When we do this, we have a better chance of becoming friends with those persons. That's good. We will actually be saying to them, "I know who you are, and you're important to me."

I'm convinced that this is why God felt it necessary that we have names. God knows our names, and that makes us important. Let's begin to see others as God sees them—each with a name and each as a very important person.

Let us pray.

Dear God: Thank you for our names and all that our names mean to us and others. Amen.

No. 34

There's More There

There is something is my bag that I want to show you, but before I can do so you must close your eyes. That's right, close your eyes and don't open them until I say so. Ready? All eyes shut?

OK. Open them. And who is this sitting in front of you? It certainly doesn't look like your pastor, does it? Of course not! But I can't fool you, for you know that beneath this awful-looking mask is the man you know as Reverend Jordan. Still, this mask gives you a startled feeling deep down inside. Right?

I hope you don't mind if I keep it on while I talk to you. Block out of your thoughts that I am behind this mask. Instead, think of it as being a strange new face in your midst, like someone new at school or a new neighbor down the street or a person who has recently joined the church. (Let me quickly say that no person who has recently joined this church looks like this.) And immediately you have a problem. Your mind can't really get behind the face to what this person is really like. You want to stop with the face and go no farther, saying to yourself, if not aloud to your friends, "I don't like that person. Ugly!" Then you do one of two things, and maybe both, when all is said and done.

First, you make fun of this person, from cruel words to a look which tells of your dislike.

Second, you keep your distance, having little or nothing to do with that person.

The one thing you didn't do was ask yourself how your actions and reactions caused that person to feel. Now, that's a very important consideration.

Granted, you're not going to meet many persons who look like this. This mask is ugly. But haven't you heard others say, and maybe you've said the same, that a particular person is ugly and because of this you should keep your distance and have as little as possible to do with that person? Maybe it isn't the face that bothers you; maybe it is a handicap or maybe it is the clothes or manners or habits or personality which causes you to turn your friendship off. If so, there are three questions to ask.

First: Is it right to treat another person this way because of how he or she looks or dresses or acts? The answer is no! Just because someone is different from us, just because that person might seem odd to us, this gives us no right whatsoever to be mean and cruel. Jesus befriended all kinds of people, many of whom were disliked by others. In fact, many criticized him for being friends to those "different" people. But we know Jesus was right. And it is right for us to do as he did.

Second: How do these actions make that person feel? The answer is "terrible!" How do we know that? Well, if someone treats us badly, we know how terrible it makes us feel. Again, we need to do as Jesus suggested, do unto others as we would have them do unto us.

And the third question: Is there any good in that other person? The answer is yes, more than we realize at first glance. There is always some good in every person, often much more than we can see from outward appearances. This is what Jesus saw in those people who had been rejected by others. And what Jesus did for those people was help them become their best selves. We must do the same.

Let me take off my mask and put it back in my bag. Remember this: Be loving in such a way that the person who might be rejected because of looks or appearance or behavior is not rejected by you.

Let us pray.

Dear God: Help us to see the good in each person no matter how he or she might look or act. Amen.

No. 35

Have a Mind of Your Own

Will you do something for me? Don't worry; it won't be hard to do. When I count to three, I want you to jump up on your feet and put your hands over your head. Here, let me show you how to do it. . . .

Now that didn't look hard, did it? Ready? On the count of three, do as I did. One, two, three. . . .

Why did you do that? Because I told you to? Sure you did. But if you had said, "Hey, I don't want to do that," do you know how I would have reacted? With a big smile! Why? Because you would have been using your own mind in deciding if jumping up was what you really wanted to do. Of course, you were having fun doing as I requested, and that's not wrong, but if you didn't want to do it, I wouldn't have been angry.

Here is one of my daughter's favorite toys. It's a jack-in-the-box. Let's turn the handle and make him jump. . . . Would you like to see him jump again?. . .

I'm reminded of the boy who didn't have a mind of his own. Whatever the other children at school or at play did, he did. And whatever his best friend wanted him to do, he did, or whatever that same friend did he wanted to do too. So it went. His mother asked why he did this, and he replied, "I don't know . . . because Jimmy did it!" And I'm reminded of the girl who hit another girl just because she was told by a friend to do it. Some friend! The boy and the girl didn't have minds of their own, or at least the minds they had weren't used as they should have been.

God wants us to be more than a jack-in-the-box or a jill-in-the-box for someone else. We are to think for ourselves.

Oh, there are times when we should do as told. For example, when our parents tell us what to do, we should obey them, for they know what is best for us. The same goes for our teachers in school. Also, there are things God wants us to do, acts of love and kindness and goodness (Jesus told us about these), and these we should do, all because they are right.

But God also wants us to use our own minds in deciding if some action is right or wrong, wise or foolish. God says to us, "Have a mind of your own! If I didn't want you to think I wouldn't have given you a mind to think with."

You will never be the kind of boy or girl God wants you to be unless you learn to think for yourself. It's an important part of growing up.

Let's turn the handle again and see Jack jump, and then let's decide not to be like him—mindless, just doing the wishes of someone else.

Have a mind of your own and use it wisely.

Let us pray.
Dear God: Help us to think for ourselves. Amen.

No. 36

All This from a Loaf of Bread and a Cup

When I say "Holy Communion," what does that mean to you?

You've seen your parents and others share in it, eating little pieces of bread and drinking some grape juice from a little cup. Ah, now you know what I'm talking about. But why do we do this?

One reason is that it helps us to remember the last meal Jesus had with his disciples. The first disciples were twelve men Jesus chose to be with him when he traveled around the country telling people about God. On the night before he was killed, he had a special meal with them. Today, we call it the Lord's Supper. When they were around the table and after they had eaten and talked of many things, Jesus did something that the disciples never forgot. And we haven't forgotten either. This is what happened.

"He took bread." Here, let me show you what he did. In my bag I have a loaf of bread. He took it in his hands like this, said a short prayer of thanks to God for the bread, and then broke it in half. After doing this he gave it to them, saying, "Take, eat."

Next, "he took a cup." Maybe that cup looked something like this one that I also have in my bag. It had in it what was called the fruit of the vine, which we are told was wine. However, here we use grape juice. We may use either one. When Jesus did this, he said a short prayer of thanks to God as he had done with the bread, and then he passed the cup to his disciples, saying, "Drink of it, all of you."

Well, since then much has been written and said about the Lord's Supper. As you grow older, I hope you will read, listen, and learn about what Jesus did then. But for now let me explain it this way.

Holy Communion is our way of remembering what Jesus meant when he broke the bread and passed the cup. The broken bread stands for his death. You see, he was willing to die, to allow his life to broken in death, if that was what he had to do in order to tell his followers and all people about God's love. So Jesus died to show God's love. And the cup stands for his life—all that he lived for. He wanted his followers to continue to live their lives as he had taught them. This we must also do.

In taking communion together, we are sharing our faith—what we believe about Jesus—with each other. Eating the bread and drinking the cup of Holy Communion is not something we normally do alone. Rather, we share with each other our faith in Jesus as the one who makes God so much more dear and near to us.

This morning your parents and others here in our church are going to eat the bread and drink from the cup, keeping all this in mind as they do it. And now you understand a little better why they are taking part in Holy Communion. There will come a time, when you're a little bit older, when you will do this too.

Let us pray.
Dear God: It is good that we can talk together about the meaning of Holy Communion. Amen.

No. 37

That's a Good Suggestion

We have something new in our church this morning. Now if you're thinking it's something big, you're wrong. It's a little smaller than a bread box, just small enough to go into my brown bag. And here it is. A suggestion box.

How many of you have ever seen a suggestion box? With no fewer hands than that going up, maybe I should ask, "What is a suggestion box?" Good; more of you put your hands up on that one. Of course, it's a box of any shape and size, and like this one it must have a pencil and paper available so that a person can write a suggestion.

The suggestion may be on any concern the person wants to share with others. After it is written, it is placed in the box. Some suggestion boxes have a long slit through which paper is put. Our suggestion box is fancier, for it has a little door at the top. All a person has to do is open it and drop the suggestion in.

Why do we want a suggestion box in our church? That's an easy question to answer. We want people to share their ideas, comments, and suggestions with the entire church. Right after I finish talking with you, an usher will take this suggestion box and put it on that big table by the front door of the sanctuary. It is hoped that by being in a place where it is seen, it will be used.

Every week, starting with this week, I will check to see what is in this suggestion box. Each and every idea, comment, and suggestion will be given serious consideration. That's right; we're very serious about this.

Some of the notes put in these boxes may be addressed to me, such as a request for me to visit a certain person, or a desire to have me preach on a certain subject, or a comment on how I can become a better pastor. And I welcome all these suggestions.

Some of the notes may pertain to other aspects of our church, like a request for us to discuss a certain concern, or a desire to have us do something in particular for others, or a comment about how the building needs fixing. There are a thousand and one suggestions for the church to consider. These will go to the moderator, to the executive council, to a committee which is directly concerned with a suggestion, and, if important enough, to the entire congregation.

Again I ask, why are we doing this? Because we want to help our church be the best church possible.

Thus, if any person, and this includes you, has a suggestion on helping this church do its job better, it should be written on one of these little pieces of paper and put it in the suggestion box. If you can't write, have your parents help you write out your suggestions. To have a better church—that's what it's all about.

Let us pray.
Dear God: Help us to make this a better church. Amen.

No. 38

No Greater Love

How many of you have seen it? "Seen what?" you ask.

About five blocks from our church is a sign nailed to a tree, a big tree in the front yard of a nice-looking house on Nevada Avenue. That sign tells the sad story of a lost dog. The sign is so big that it is hard to miss. Have any of you seen it? Well, for those who haven't seen it yet, yesterday I parked my car by the curb of that house just long enough to draw on a piece of paper how that sign looks. Then, when I got home, I drew it on a larger piece of paper. You guessed it; it's in my brown bag. And here it is.

On both the left and right is the same word: Lost. Across the top in bold letters is this word: WANTED. Underneath that is: MALE IRISH SETTER. (Ah, that is one of my favorite kinds of dog, a real beauty!) Then the sign says: Belongs to very sad children. And under that is a very sad face with turned down mouth and big tears falling from the eyes. On the left side of the sign it reads: He is big/He loves Bridget/He loves Molly. Under this is written: Please return him. On the right side is written: REWARD. At the bottom is the phone number.

When I first saw this sign, and again as I copied it down on paper, it took me back many, many years, when I too lost my dog. Inky was his name. He was a gift from some passing motorist. By this I mean that we lived just far enough from town that many unwanted pets were abandoned near us, many of which I think we fed and cared for. But Inky was special. When we lost him, we knew what happened to him. He was killed—by a car.

You can imagine how sad I was, and in one sense I am still sad. I loved that dog.

Right now Bridget and Molly are wondering what has happened to their dog. Most likely he is still alive somewhere. They have put up a sign hoping that someone has him and wants to return him, and they want it known that the Irish setter belongs to them. Their plea: Please Return Him.

There is an old saying that goes like this: "A man's best friend is his dog." The same goes for girls and boys too. Why? Because between us and our dogs is a love that is endearing and wonderful, expressed with a pat on the head and with a wag of the tail; both actions say so very much about the relationship between us. If you have a dog at home, you know what this means.

The sign also reminded me of how deep our love for a dog can be; and if Bridget and Molly or you and I love our dogs this way, how much more must God love us. We are more important to God than our dogs are to us. Loving our dogs as we do, this is saying a lot—that God cares much more for us.

When did God start loving us like this? From the day we were born, continuing to love us until the day we die! And after that God will continue to love us—forever.

I hope Bridget and Molly will soon have their dog back, for they love him very much. And I hope we never forget how much God loves us too, for there is no greater love than this.

Let us pray.
Dear God: Thank you for loving us like you do. Amen.

No. 39

The Cafeteria of Life

Just one minute please. I have to get ready. First, out of my bag comes a napkin for my lap, then a knife and a fork, the knife in one hand, the fork in the other. Now I'm ready to talk about something I did yesterday.

How many of you have eaten at a cafeteria? What is a cafeteria? It's a kind of restaurant where instead of first sitting down, looking at a menu, and telling the waitress or waiter what you want, you choose food already prepared. If many people are there, you have to stand in line and wait your turn to select your food.

All this is fresh in my mind because yesterday we had out-of-town company (relatives), and they took us to a cafeteria which had just opened in our city. As I sat there after the meal, thinking and talking about all the good food we had just eaten, I decided this cafeteria experience has a lesson about life. It has to do with making decisions.

"What are you going to have?" I can't remember ever going to a cafeteria without being asked that question. At that moment I was faced with a decision. The first person behind the counter who was in charge of the salads said, "Can I help you?" There were about fifteen different salads to choose from. At that moment I had to decide what I wanted because other people were lined up behind me and they didn't want me to stand there all day as I made up my mind. The same thing happened several times as I moved down the line.

Isn't this the way life is—ever moving us on and all the while requiring us to make decisions?

It is important that we make wise decisions. What we choose both in the cafeteria and in the rest of life becomes part of us. So we try to choose foods that make for a balanced diet, ranging from vegetables to meats to dairy products. That makes good health sense. If we only chose starchy foods, like potatoes, or only sweets, like pie, it would not be good for our health. What we become will depend much on what we choose. For example, the right kinds of foods are going to make us strong and healthy. The same goes not only for food but for every area of life, like attitudes, friends, reading material, and activities. Yes, what we take in becomes us, so we must decide wisely.

As I neared the end of the line, I found myself wishing I had chosen fish instead of chicken and dumplings. But the decision was made and I couldn't go back and change it. I had to live with my choice, like it or not. Next time I will make a different choice. So goes life. We make mistakes, to be sure, but let us learn from those mistakes and choose more wisely the next time.

One more thought. Life is ever pushing us to make decisions. Isn't it wonderful that we have been given the privilege of making choices in the first place? God thought it was important that we have this freedom to decide for ourselves. But if we are to do God's will, we need to learn how to use this freedom of choice. That is going to require decision-making at its best, and that is never easy. But then God didn't make life easy!

Let us pray.

Dear God: Not only do we thank you for giving us the right to make decisions, but we pray for help in making them, so that our decisions might be right ones. Amen.

No. 40

Tuning in on Unity

Throughout the world today, churches are doing something special. They are observing Worldwide Communion Sunday.

While many of us belong to different churches (or I should say different denominations, such as Baptist, Methodist, Presbyterian, Catholic, Episcopal, and United Church of Christ), we are still stressing in our prayers and actions that we want more unity among all the churches. When we say we want more unity, we mean that we belong together, that we want to do more things together. Do you know what this wish for unity does for me? It gives me a good feeling. Let me tell you why.

One of the great things the church does (and when all is said and done it really is the greatest thing it does) is bring people together to worship God. Together we have a better opportunity to understand God.

So, when we talk about this kind of church unity, we emphasize what we should remember every Sunday, that there are many Christians beyond our local church who are doing what we are doing. There is a kind of togetherness we need to feel and remember, for we must share together our faith in God.

You know, right here in our city at this very minute there are also other Christians worshiping God. It gives me a good feeling to know this. Let me show you one of the ways I know this is happening. I have brought my radio in my brown bag. By turning it on and tuning it just right, we can hear the worship service at the First Presbyterian Church. Listen. If I turn the dial a little farther, we can hear the worship service at the First

Baptist Church. There. And on another station we can hear the congregation of the First United Methodist Church worshiping God. Good. Yes, we may be in different churches, but we are worshiping the same God, and that makes me feel good.

But all of this doesn't stop with us here in our city. Around the world there are also many Christians worshiping God, and we need to remember that we are together in this desire for more unity. In a real sense we are a big family that is widely scattered around the world. It would be sad if we were to forget about one another. But how glad it makes us to realize that we belong together, that we are all members of God's family.

Yes, we are not alone in our worship of God. This special emphasis on Worldwide Communion Sunday helps us to remember this important truth. This is what God wants. This is how the Bible says it: "Finally, all of you, have unity of spirit."

All the churches that are participating in Worldwide Communion Sunday will today take part in Holy Communion, will talk about what all this means, and will pray that God will help us to have more unity as Christians.

Let us pray.
Dear God: Help us all to be united as your people, ever ready to work together in doing your will. Amen.

No. 41

There's Something About Those Cobwebs

No bag this morning. As you know, I normally bring my brown bag with something in it. It's called a prop.

I have a prop this morning, but there was no way to get it into my bag. No, it isn't too big. Rather, I can't reach it. Furthermore, if I could reach it, it most likely would tear up before I could get it here this morning.

Oh, it is here this morning. Right here in this sanctuary. I see it every Sunday morning. Where I sit in my big chair on the other side of the pulpit, I can't help but see it. Do you see it? Of course not, you can't see it by looking this way. It's behind you. No, not right behind you, nor is it where your parents and friends are seated. Look above them. Do you see it? Wait a minute, how can you see it when you don't know what you're looking for? Let me point it out to you.

Do you see those three little stained-glass windows above the big round stained-glass window? See anything in those windows? When the sun is just right, and it usually is just right this time in the morning, you can see some cobwebs in them, especially in the one on your right. That's what I'm talking about.

Now you can see why I couldn't put that cobweb in my bag. Not only is that little window a good forty or fifty feet up there, but did you ever hear of anyone putting a cobweb in a brown bag? I haven't.

Because that cobweb is there week after week doesn't mean that our janitor doesn't do his job. Even if he saw it up there, how would he get up to brush it away? Maybe I'm the only one who has ever seen it. After all, on Sunday mornings I'm always looking that way when everyone else, except the choir, is looking this way.

Those cobwebs say something to me every Sunday morning. Although the sanctuary is cleaned for our use on Sundays, those cobwebs are still there. What this says to me is that while I may be good in many ways, yet some of the wrongs I don't want in my life may still be there. My desire to be better is all well and good, but those cobwebs up there remind me of the wrongs I've committed in the past.

Some of those wrongs may have harmed others, and I've never gone to those I've harmed to ask for forgiveness, to allow them to say to me, "It's OK now." At times I have sinned against God—and by this I mean that I haven't allowed God's ways to be my ways; rather I've insisted on doing what God didn't want me to do—and I haven't yet accepted the forgiveness offered, allowing God to say, "It's OK now." Those cobwebs remind me of that.

Just as those cobwebs are difficult to get rid of, so are many of my wrongs. I need help. Only forgiveness can brush away the cobwebs in my life. So my thoughts about those cobwebs conclude that I need to see what I've done wrong and that I need to know there is help to do something about it.

Let us pray.
Dear God: Brush the cobwebs of wrongs from our lives with forgiveness. Amen.

No. 42

Oihcconip

I've brought a friend along with me this morning. This friend is special to me, for I made him. That's right, I made him. What kind of friend could this possibly be? Let's find out. He is in my bag.

It's a puppet. And, as you can see, this puppet isn't an *it*. A "he" would be a better label. His name is Oihcconip, which is the backward spelling of Pinocchio. You know the story of Pinocchio, don't you? Well, my puppet is nothing more and nothing less than a puppet made out of cardboard colored with crayons. When I pull the strings tied to his arms, they move the arms. The same is true of his legs. He is that simple. He couldn't do anything without my pulling on these strings.

Oh, how I wish he weren't so dependent on me! I would like to be able to cut these strings and have him run around like a real, live boy, as Pinocchio did in the story. But then he might get into trouble like Pinocchio did, and that would make me sad. That is the chance I will have to take if my little puppet will ever become a real, live boy. Of course, we're only making believe.

You know, God made us, and that is a real story. Did God make us to be like puppets? No! We don't have strings on us! God wants us to be real, live boys and girls. And it is important to God that we learn how to be responsible for what we do.

To be sure, there was a time in our lives when we weren't like this, when someone else had to take care of us. We might say it this way: we had strings on us. I'm not talking about real strings. When we were babies and very small children, we were very dependent upon our parents. They helped us do what we couldn't do for ourselves. In a very loving way they controlled our lives. But they don't want to do this forever. So as we begin to grow older and are able to assume more responsibilities, they cut those invisible strings, thus giving us more and more freedom.

Now with this pair of scissors I can cut these strings on Oihcconip, but see what happens. He falls down in a heap. The reason, of course, is that he doesn't have life. But *we* have life, and when our parents cut us loose they are giving us the freedom to be ourselves, to stand on our own feet and live as God wants us to.

God doesn't want us to be human puppets with our every movement controlled by others, even loving parents. God's wish for us is that when we are old enough the controlling strings we experience when very young will be cut. The strings are cut by simply letting us grow up and giving us freedom of choice. The older we get, the more decisions we have to make on our own. That's important to God, to our parents, and to us.

But with our freedom we can get into trouble. Many have misused their freedom, thus hurting not only themselves but others. We call that *sin*. But we can also do a great deal of good with our freedom. God doesn't keep us from doing bad things. Neither does God force us to do good things. In fact, God took a risk in giving us freedom of choice. We have to choose which it will be, good or bad. Sometimes we will choose the bad; God hopes we will choose the good.

The strings have been cut. How do we choose to use our freedom?

Let us pray.
Dear God: Thank you for our freedom, for it means so much to us. Amen.

No. 43

We've Come a Long Way

I wonder what it's going to be like a hundred years from now. Try as hard as I can to think that far ahead, I must admit that I don't know. That is not an easy thing to figure out. A hundred years is a long time. Times change so quickly. There is simply no telling what life is going to be like a hundred years from now.

I wonder if the people who lived a hundred years ago tried to imagine what it would be like today. I don't know. But I'm sure about one thing. If they were here to see what we see, they would see things that they could never have imagined. For example, they didn't have cars. Instead, they used real horse power, either riding a horse or having the horse (or horses) pull a carriage or wagon, to go places. Now we have cars all around us. The speed we go in a car, even at fifty-five miles an hour, would have scared them to death.

Or again, they would be surprised at how we dress. When I look at the pictures of how people dressed back then, I feel so much more comfortable, for they look so uncomfortable. Yes, they would be surprised and shocked at how much less we wear.

And again, the thought of someone going to the moon, especially even before the airplane had been invented, much less a rocket, was simply unthinkable for most people then. Impossible is most likely the word they would have used if told it would happen someday.

These examples show how hard it was for people a hundred years ago to imagine what life would be like today. And the same is so for us in looking ahead a hundred years from now.

97

But there was one thing a few people felt pretty confident of a hundred years ago. It was this church. You see, they didn't start this church by thinking that in twenty-five or fifty or seventy-five years the people of this church would close its doors and this building would then cease being used for a church. No way! Rather, they were expecting this church—the First Congregational Church—to continue on and on and on, being a church for as long as Colorado Springs is here.

Well, they were right about the first hundred years. We are still here worshiping God and helping people to live better. Sure, many things have changed during this time, mainly in the way we live. There have even been some changes in the way the church does its work. Still, the church is trying to do what God wants, and that is what the founders of this church envisioned that it would be doing today.

Yes, today, this Sunday, is a special day. It's our one-hundredth birthday. We've come a long way. Let's do a little celebrating.

For the occasion, I've made myself a birthday hat, and I have it in my bag. It has on it the words HAPPY BIRTHDAY, with the number 100 in red. Also, I have this, which I didn't make but it's for celebrating at a birthday party—a party blower. I'm ready. Let's sing "HAPPY BIRTHDAY" to our church. When we come to the part where we say the name, just say "to our church." Here we go.

Happy birthday to you,
Happy birthday to you,
Happy birthday to our church,
Happy birthday to you.

You know, I have the feeling that God was singing along with us.

Let us pray.
Dear God: Thank you for letting us celebrate our church's one-hundredth birthday. Amen.

No. 44

The Church's Holy Ghost

We sing it every Sunday. It's found in our hymnbook. In my brown bag I have a hymnbook; and I'm going to sing it to you. As I sing it, listen carefully for any words that remind you of Halloween. It goes like this.

> Praise God from whom all blessings flow;
> Praise Him, all creatures here below;
> Praise Him above, ye heavenly host;
> Praise Father, Son, and Holy Ghost.
> Amen.

That is called the Doxology. We sing it when the ushers bring the offering up to the altar.

Frequently, but not every Sunday, we also sing this:

> Glory be to the Father, and to the Son, and to the Holy Ghost; as it was in the beginning, is now, and ever shall be, world without end, Amen, Amen.

That is called the Gloria Patri. We sing it after reading together from the Old Testament book of Psalms. Gloria Patri—it sounds like a girl's name, doesn't it? Started back in the days of the early church, its purpose is to turn a Jewish psalm into a Christian act of praise.

Now I didn't sing these two musical responses to demonstrate why the choir doesn't want me to sing with them. They do better without me. Rather, I sang them so that you could hear the word that reminds us of Halloween. When you heard me say "ghost," what did that mean to you?

99

A minister friend of mine some years ago told me that his little girl announced one Sunday she wasn't going to church anymore. When asked why, she said, "Because they sing about ghosts there."

This week is Halloween. It's a lot of fun to talk about ghosts, to dress up like ghosts, to scare and to be scared. Right?

But is this what we are talking and singing about in church? "Holy Ghost." Of course not! Well then, why do we use that word? Back hundreds of years ago, it was a word used with no thought of Halloween in mind. It meant "Spirit." When they spoke of the Holy God we talk about in church today, they used the words "Holy Ghost." You see, they were not talking about some kind of spook that we naturally think about on Halloween. Rather, they were talking about God who is unseen with our eyes but who is very much part of our lives, the One who gives us life, the One who goes with us throughout life.

I agree that it is confusing to say "Ghost" when we mean "Spirit." So why do we do it? Because the songs are very old; the words (host and ghost) rhyme; and by custom we have kept them as they were first used in the church hundreds of years ago.

But now we know what we are singing in church when we sing "Holy Ghost." And it isn't a "what" but is instead a "Who"—it is the Holy Spirit, the God and Creator of us all, who is with us all.

Let us pray.
Dear God: Help us to know the meaning of the words in songs we sing about you. Amen.

No. 45

Just Plain Water

In my bag I have a bottle of water. Here, take a look at it. Does it look like special water to you? It isn't. It's just plain water. But with this water we are going to do something special.

In a few minutes I'm going to use this water in a way that was used for most of you when you were small. We call it infant baptism.

About a week ago, I was asked to baptize a small child. Of course, I was happy to say I would. And we are going to baptize this child this morning. This is how it is done.

First, the parents will bring their child and stand with me in front of the congregation. Then, I will repeat some words Jesus said: "Let the children come to me, and do not hinder them; for to such belongs the kingdom of heaven." (Jesus loved all children!) Next, I will say some things about baptism and explain why we do it.

I will then ask the parents some questions, such as: "Will you promise to teach your child what the Bible says, when your child is old enough to understand?" "Will you live in such a way that this child will learn how to be good by watching you?" "Will you tell your child what it means to be a Christian as well as the meaning of prayer and church membership?" After this, I will ask the members of this church if they will help these parents perform these duties.

When all this has been said, I will say a short prayer asking for God's special blessing on these parents and this child. Finally, I will take the child in my arms and put some of this water on the child's head, saying as I do this,

"I baptize you in the name of the Father, and of the Son, and of the Holy Spirit. Amen."

Notice I said that I was going to put some of this water on the baby's head. In a few minutes the senior deacon will put this water into the baptismal font. Why use this water? We already know that it's just plain water. I took if from the faucet in the church kitchen. Well, the kind of water we use or how it is used isn't what is important. The water is only a symbol, and a symbol is something that tells us about something else. In this case, use of water sugggests cleaning something. No, this isn't another way of giving this child a bath. Well then, what does all this mean?

First, we all belong to God, even the youngest of us.

Second, our parents help us to understand God's love. They bring us to the church for baptism, and in the baptism the water is used to say that our parents, along with the people in the church, promise to help us learn how to live a life that is cleansed—made clean—of what is wrong in life. This makes it possible for us to know more fully the love God has for us.

And third, this love is a gift to us without our even asking for it. Granted, this child doesn't know what we are doing this morning. I don't know if this child will cry, but to hear some of them cry, obviously they think something worse is going on. But in time this child will learn, and when old enough, will (hopefully) accept what these parents and the church are doing this morning. But remember this: the baptizing of small children reminds us that God agreed to love us even before we knew it or could respond to it. When we baptize, we start the process by which this child will learn about the love of God.

I know you will want to watch closely as we baptize this child.

Let us pray.

Dear God: As we watch this baptism, remembering what we have said about it, help us to understand more fully why we do it. Amen.

No. 46

It Makes Cents

When you get your allowance, how do you spend it? As fast as you can? Sure, that's one way of doing it. But there is another way, a better way, to spend your money.

You start with a pencil and a piece of paper, writing down the important things on which you should spend your money. This is called budgeting. Surely you have seen your parents do this. If you don't budget, you can get in trouble with your money.

Let's say you get a dollar a week in allowance (I wish I had gotten this much when I was your age, and some of you may be saying to yourselves that you wish you got that much now). You get your allowance, and you rush out to spend the whole dollar on bubble gum. Now out of that dollar you were supposed to buy such things as pencils for school, save some of it, and give some of it to the church (say about ten cents). Well, if you didn't plan what part of that dollar was to go where, you would come up short. Your parents wouldn't be very happy, would they?

The church also has to budget the money it gets. Your parents are meeting this morning after the worship service to decide on next year's budget. Each year the church must make out a budget or else it might not spend its money as it should. That would be sad, and it would cause a big problem. Let me illustrate how the church is planning to spend its money this coming year. Of course, this can only be done by your parents and the other church members voting to spend the money this way.

103

Let's take that dollar again as the basis of this explanation. To help out I've brought in my brown bag a dollar I made myself. It's really big, like four feet by two feet! Since this isn't a real dollar, I'm sure you won't get terribly upset when I cut it up. When you go home today, don't you cut up a real dollar bill like I'm going to cut up this fake one, or I'll really be in trouble with your parents.

Now, for every dollar given to this church for this coming year, about sixty cents will go for the current local church's expenses, such as, salaries for those who work for the church, utilities (lights and water and gas), office supplies (paper, ink, stamps, plus other needs), and church school supplies (books, crayons, films, and things like this). That totals in all _____¢. So let's cut off this much.

Out of the same dollar about twenty-two cents is for the costs of the building, paying back the people who loaned us the money to build it, along with the money we need to pay them for letting us borrow this money. That totals in all _____¢. So let's cut off this much.

Out of this dollar we give nine cents to the support of our state conference, helping our church throughout the state to work better helping people. That total is _____¢. So let's cut off this much.

Also, to our denomination we give nine cents out of this same dollar, this money going to help our church do its work in our country and world. And that total is _____¢. So that's how we spend the remaining part.

And that is how each dollar given to our church is spent.

Of course, other monies are given by our church for good causes like: One Great Hour of Sharing, Neighbors in Need, American Indian offering, and FISH (that's a local group of people who help people in need). These monies come by way of gifts which the church passes on to where they should go.

104

From whom does the church get its money? Your parents, friends of the church, and from you and me too. We all must give willingly and happily. And we all need to remember Paul's words, "God loves a cheerful giver." That's right! But God also asks us all—including the church—how we are spending the money given to us. How do we each answer?

Let us pray.
Dear God: Help us to spend our money wisely. Amen.

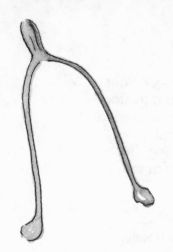

No. 47

A Pully-bone and a Wish

There is one part of the turkey that is extra special to me—the wishbone.

When I was growing up I called it the pully-bone. It's that forked bone found in the breast of a bird. Since we usually eat turkey on Thanksgiving, and since it is such a large bird, its pully-bone is just right. I have one in my brown bag.

Every Thanksgiving, after we had all eaten our fill of turkey, dressing, gravy, candied yams, cranberry sauce, and hot rolls, my brother and I would ask for the pully-bone. He would take hold of one side, and I the other. "Make a wish," we would say, and then each would pull. Many of you have done this, so you already know what happens. It breaks, but never in the middle. The one with the biggest piece hopes the wish will come true. The way we did it, we had to make our wish to ourselves, for if we told the other what we wanted that meant it might not come true. It was and still is a lot of fun to do. This coming Thursday is Thanksgiving Day, and my son and I will carry on this pully-bone tradition.

"Make a wish." We all like to do this, whether or not we tell anyone what our wish is. I venture to say that you have a lot of wishes. You may have been playing at a friend's house yesterday and come home saying, "I want that kind of toy." You shake your piggy bank and sigh, "I wish my parents would give me more allowance." You get your report card and wishfully moan, "If only I could be as smart as Johnny or Mary." You do not want to go to school tomorrow, so you long for bad weather, saying

"I want it to snow the school doors shut." You get sick, and this keeps you from doing what you want to do, so you declare, "I want to get well—*now!*" There is seemingly no end to the list of our wishes and wants. Some of what we want will probably happen. And some wishes may be impossible dreams and not happen. It's important for us to look at our wishes honestly.

The best place to begin is to understand what God's wishes for us are. God has been good to all of us, giving us many more blessings than we can possibly count. In our better moments we all know this to be true. That should be the main reason we have a Thanksgiving Day, to say "thank you" to God.

Let's make this our wish this Thanksgiving when we pull the pully-bone. But why just on Thanksgiving Day? Why not on every day of the year with or without a pully-bone?

Let us pray.
Dear God: We are thankful. Amen.

No. 48

For the Birds

It happened this past week. It snowed. Not only did it snow, but it turned icy and got very, very cold. I shiver just thinking about it. As a result, last Tuesday most of us got an unexpected holiday from school and work. Even I stayed home on that day—I had to! I stayed in by the fire, played games with the family, ate popcorn, and did some reading. But every time I looked out the window, I shivered.

That bad weather did more than just make me shiver. It made me worry. I didn't worry for myself, for I was being taken care of very well. No, the weather outside made me concerned about the birds. I worried about how they were getting along. The trees across the street from my house looked so cold and icy. The ground was covered, and so was the food supply the birds depended upon. The wind was sharp and biting and it occurred to me that opening their wings to fly must have made the birds shiver and not want to fly. And I must say that I didn't see many birds flying that day.

And I did more than worry. I put out bird food—seed, bread, and suet. Do you know what suet is? This is a hard animal fat, and the birds really like it. I have some in my brown bag for you to see. This is what I was feeding the birds.

I understand that last Sunday some of you made bird feeders out of pipe cleaners in church school; that you strung Cheerios on the pipe cleaners and shaped them so you could hang them on a tree limb. That's good. I'm sure the birds liked it, especially last Tuesday. You were doing your part in helping the birds.

But with so much snow, and with that snow covering up so much of their food, I felt something more should be done. With my family's help, I put a plate of bread and suet on the back patio. Unfortunately, the birds didn't get it—a stray dog ate it for breakfast. I wonder if it was a bird dog!

Should I have worried as I did? I think I worried too much. Don't get me wrong, for I know I did the right thing. We all should care for God's creatures when we can.

I question now whether in my concern for the birds last Tuesday I was aware of what God was doing for them—more than I was. God gave them the ability to survive that cold day and even colder days. God loves birds too. Remember how Jesus talked about the birds? He commented that they didn't "sow nor reap nor gather into barns," and yet God takes care of them. That's a comforting thought.

But you know, in talking about the birds, Jesus said something else, something about us, right after he had spoken about the birds: "Are you not of more value than they?" We're more important than the birds, and God dearly loves the birds. This being so, think how much God must love us. That's a comforting thought too.

Let us pray.
Dear God: We know that you care not only for us but also for the birds, and this makes us happy. Amen.

No. 49

Hurt Not

May I tell you something that is to be held in confidence? By this I mean that what I'm about to tell you is to be only between you and me. It's personal and rather embarrassing. If you won't tell anybody, I'll share it with you.

It happened when I was in the second grade. There was this girl. Everyone made fun of her, and I was no different from the rest. I made fun of her too, even though I knew it was the wrong thing to do.

Well, one day when several of us were making fun of her, she did something to us. She stuck out her tongue. Like this. That simply egged us on. No, it wasn't an egg I used; rather, it was a rock. I picked up a rock, much like this one I have in my bag, and I threw it at her.

Now, my parents had told me never to throw rocks at other people, and I knew it was wrong. But I was so mad that I just forgot their advice.

Fortunately, she saw it coming and turned at just the right time. Instead of hitting her on the head, it hit her on the back. Nevertheless, it hurt. She started crying and ran home.

And I started running home too. Was I scared! Yes, I knew it was wrong to hit someone with a rock, but now it was too late to "unthrow" that rock.

It was only a few minutes before our telephone rang. It was Jackie's mother. Was she mad! And in less than a minute after my mother finished talking to Jackie's mother, she called me in. I told her what had happened. Then I said that I was truly sorry for what I had done.

Mother told me that if I really was sorry, I should go tell Jackie so. I just stood there and shook my head, saying, "I can't do that."

Mothers have a way of making their point. Mine sure did! When that was settled, we went to see Jackie. Yes, Mother went with me down the alley and up to Jackie's back door. I knocked. Both she and her mother answered the door. I told her that I was sorry and that I was wrong in what I had done. Would she forgive me? She did.

Through the years, I haven't forgotten that hurting experience. The lesson I learned then and still remember is that I couldn't really be forgiven for what I had done wrong until I had confessed my wrong and sought to make amends—to right the wrong. That is an important lesson to learn.

We may not hurt someone with a rock like I did. More often we try to hurt others with words or actions or neglect. We know when we hurt others, and they know what we are trying to do when we do it. And we're wrong every time we do it. The lesson we must learn is not to hurt. And when we do hurt someone, we must say so and try our best to right the wrong.

Today Jackie and I are good friends. This is what God wants us to be with everyone—friends. For this to happen, we know what we must do.

Let us pray.

Dear God: We don't want to hurt others, but when we do, help us to know how to make the wrong right. Amen.

No. 50

I Want for Christmas

What are you going to get this Christmas? You don't know? Maybe I should ask: What do you want to get this Christmas? That you know!

Perhaps you feel like Dennis the Menace, as shown in the comic section of the newspaper a few days ago. Dennis was sitting on Santa Claus's knee in a big department store looking and pointing in every direction and saying as fast as he could, ". . . an' one of them, an' some of those, an' one of them, an' two of those, an'. . ." Have you done that yet?

Or you may have done the next best thing by getting your hands on what I have in my brown bag this morning, a catalog. Ah, this is more than a catalog, it's a wish book. I can still remember when I was young, your age, spending hours looking at all the many, many toys that this book offered for sale. With a pencil, I would mark which ones I really wanted and show them to Dad and Mom, saying what Dennis the Menace said. How many of you do this too? Just as I suspected, it's still a wish book.

But I didn't get everything I wanted. Oh, under the Christmas tree on Christmas morning, I found many of the toys I had asked for, some from Dad and Mom and others with a card reading "From Santa." Looking back, I would have to say that I was a very fortunate little boy, getting more than I should have. But I didn't argue about it.

Yet, there were those other toys marked in the catalog that didn't come to me. Dad and Mom could have given those to me if they had wanted to. Knowing this and being a normal little boy, I sometimes questioned their love for me when I didn't get everything I wanted. Only with the wisdom of age can I now say that by not giving me all I asked for showed an even deeper love for me. At the time, that was hard to understand. They loved me by knowing and giving what was best for me.

The same is true in the life we live between our many Christmases. We don't get everything we want, do we? Yet in our prayers we hear ourselves telling God of our many wants and needs. Most assuredly we are heard. And if we stop to think about it, God has been very good to us, giving us far more than we can give thanks for.

How do we know this? There is another book we must learn to read, not at all like the catalog. It is the Bible. It says, "Therefore do not be anxious, saying, 'What shall we eat?' or 'What shall we drink?' or 'What shall we wear?' " And why does it say this? Because God knows that you need them all. Not only do we know that God is aware of our needs, but we believe also that God will give us what we really need, that is, if we will receive what is given to us.

During this season of the year we need to give thanks for God's special gift to us. That gift is Jesus, whose birthday we celebrate at Christmas time.

Let us pray.
Dear God: While we will receive many things we think we need this Christmas, may we receive with joy the special gift you give us, knowing that we do need Jesus in our lives. Amen.

No. 51

It's a Birthday Party

Christmas Day—December 25—is just a few days away. You know that without my having to tell you, right? Already you have been thinking and planning for Christmas, and you're not the only ones doing this. We adults are also preparing for it.

Every Christmas creates a lot of excitement. Everywhere we turn we see signs of this important day, causing us to say as my son said the other day, "I can't wait." We go shopping and we see the store windows filled with toys, games, and other gifts. All around us are the lights of Christmas. Wherever we go, the music of Christmas is heard, like "Joy to the World," "O Little Town of Bethlehem," and "Hark! the Herald Angels Sing." And there are many more things that help to remind us of this coming day so full of excitement and expectation, such as bells, holly wreaths, manger scenes, Christmas trees, ornaments, mistletoe, and candles. Yes, all these and more are the signs of Christmas.

That first Christmas, however, was different. There weren't any of the things I have just mentioned. No, not one. It happened in a different way and in a different place. In a stable, a place where cattle and horses were kept, a child was born. His name was Jesus. What made the people happy then was the awareness of what this child meant to them. They saw that in the birth of Jesus, God was doing something very special. So they celebrated. And the people who have believed this since then have also celebrated.

Today we have many signs of Jesus' birth, signs that weren't even thought of then, such as Christmas trees, lights, candles, and bells. But that's all right! Still we celebrate his birth by remembering what it means to us.

What we have done is add our own special touch to this celebration. In our own way it has become a birthday party. Since this is so, I think we should go one step farther in our celebration. The people didn't have a cake, but I think it's most fitting to have one today—for Jesus' birthday. And that's what we have this morning. Underneath this brown bag is a cake. My family and I baked a cake for this occasion. And here it is. Since we're celebrating the first birthday Jesus had, let's put one candle on and light it. Amy, will you be the one to blow it out? Immediately after the worship service we're going to cut this cake and give everyone a piece.

I want to encourage you to have a birthday cake for Jesus at your home on either Christmas Eve or on Christmas Day. Ask if you can help bake one.

Remember—Christmas Day is Jesus' birthday.

Let us pray.
Dear God: Help us celebrate Jesus' birthday as we should. Amen.

No. 52

A Rock and a Friend

Suppose you had a friend who was moving away; how would you feel? Or you might be the one moving away; how would you feel? Sad? Sure you would. Whenever friends are forced to part company, it's anything but a happy time. Of course, this doesn't mean that you stop being friends, but it does mean that you won't get to see each other as often as before. And that's what makes it a very sad time.

Why am I talking about all this? Because we're friends. We've been friends for many years. I've been your friend as well as your minister. This coming week my family and I are moving away. I'm going to be a minister in another church in another state many, many miles from here. This is my last Sunday here, my last time to talk with you like this. While I'm looking forward to my new job, still I'm sad that it has come time for me to move away. It's always a sad time to move away from friends.

But this will not mean the end of our friendship. That's why I want to give each of you something. It's not very big and it doesn't cost anything, except it did take some time to find. How many of you have ever heard of a friendship rock? That is what I want to give you.

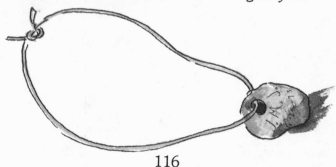

What is it? It's a small rock that has a hole in it. Through this hole you put a string and tie the ends of the string. It's important that the string be long enough to go over the head and around the neck. Here, it's better to show one to you than to just tell you about it.

Where do you find these rocks? There are more around than you might think. I would say that each of us has walked past hundreds, maybe thousands, in our lives. The best place to find large numbers of them together is in a creek, because the water helps to make the little holes. What happens is that over a long period of time the water washes away the softer part of the rock, thus leaving the hole. By the way, that is where I found this friendship rock. I found some for you too.

Not only have I tied each with a string so that you can put it around your neck, I've also done something special to each rock. With a certain kind of ink, called india marking ink, I've written my initials on each one, with today's date. Here in my bag I have many, for I want each of you to have one.

Each time you look at or feel this friendship rock, remember some of the things we have learned together as friends, about God, Jesus, love, kindness, honesty, the church. But also remember that our friendship has not ended. Allow me to say it the way it's said in the Bible: "It is right for me to feel thus about you all, because I hold you in my heart."

Let us pray.

Dear God: May the friendship we have never end. Amen.